The Riddles Standard Types in Traffic

'Steam Past' Books from Allen & Unwin

THE LIMITED by O. S. Nock
THE BIRTH OF BRITISH RAIL by Michael R. Bonavia
STEAM'S INDIAN SUMMER by George Heiron and Eric Treacy
GRAVEYARD OF STEAM by Brian Handley
PRESERVED STEAM IN BRITAIN by Patrick B. Whitehouse
MEN OF THE GREAT WESTERN by Peter Grafton
TRAVELLING BY TRAIN IN THE EDWARDIAN AGE by Philip Unwin
MAUNSELL'S NELSONS by D. W. Winkworth
MAN OF THE SOUTHERN: JIM EVANS LOOKS BACK by Jim Evans
TRAINS TO NOWHERE: BRITISH STEAM TRAIN ACCIDENTS 1923–1960 by J. A. B. Hamilton
TRAVELLING BY TRAIN IN THE 'TWENTIES AND 'THIRTIES by Philip Unwin
MEN OF THE LNER by Peter Grafton
A HISTORY OF THE LMS by O. S. Nock: I. The First Years, 1923–30
A HISTORY OF THE LNER by Michael R. Bonavia: I. The Early Years, 1923–33
ON AND OFF THE RAILS by Sir John Elliot
THE RIDDLES STANDARD TYPES IN TRAFFIC by G. Freeman Allen

STEAM, a year book edited by Roger Crombleholme and Terry Kirtlanc

The Riddles Standard Types in Traffic

G. Freeman Allen

London
GEORGE ALLEN & UNWIN
Boston Sydney

**George Allen & Unwin (Publishers) Ltd,
40 Museum Street, London WC1A 1LU, UK**

George Allen & Unwin (Publishers) Ltd,
Park Lane, Hemel Hempstead, Herts HP2 4TE, UK

Allen & Unwin Inc.,
9 Winchester Terrace, Winchester, Mass 01890, USA

George Allen & Unwin Australia Pty Ltd,
8 Napier Street, North Sydney, NSW 2060, Australia

First published in 1982

British Library Cataloguing in Publication Data

Allen, Geoffrey Freeman
The Riddles standard types in traffic.
1. Riddles, Robert Arthur 2. Locomotives –
Great Britain
I. Title
625.2'61'0924 TJ603.4.G7
ISBN 0–04–385092–8

Set in 10 on 12 point Bembo by Nene Phototypesetters Ltd
and printed in Great Britain
by Biddles Ltd, Guildford, Surrey

Contents

	List of Illustrations		*page* 11
	Author's Preface		13
1	Genesis		15
2	The Class 7 Pacifics		20
3	The Class 6 Pacifics		38
4	The Class 8 Pacific		44
5	The Mixed Traffic 4–6–0s		51
6	The Moguls		69
7	The Tank Engines		76
8	The Class 9 2–10–0s		89
	Appendix 1	BR Standard Steam Locomotives: Leading Particulars	106
	Appendix 2	BR Standard Steam Locomotive Tender Types	107
	Appendix 3	Construction Dates and Locomotive Works Responsible	108
	Index		109

Illustrations

1	Pacific no. 70001, 'Lord Hurcomb'	*page* 21
2	No. 70003, 'John Bunyan', on the down 'Norfolkman'	22
3	'William Shakespeare' and the SR 'Golden Arrow' at Victoria	23
4	'Alfred the Great' and the 'Bournemouth Belle'	24
5	No. 70043 accelerating past Kilburn	26
6	Britannia Pacific no. 70025, 'Western Star'	28
7	No. 70045, 'Lord Rowallan', heading the up 'Waverley'	30
8	No. 70041, 'Sir John Moore', with the 6.50 pm from King's Cross	31
9	No. 70035, 'Rudyard Kipling', with the Grimsby–Whitland fish train	32
10	Sad spectacle: no. 70000, 'Britannia'	34
11	Two Britannias double-heading a Saturday extra	36
12	Class 6 4–6–2 no. 72000, 'Clan Buchanan', as built	39
13	No. 72004, 'Clan Macdonald'	40
14	No. 72007, 'Clan Mackintosh', takes water at Ayr	42
15	Unique class 8 4–6–2 no. 71000, 'Duke of Gloucester'	45
16	The 'Duke' undergoing tests	47
17	The 'Duke' at work	49
18	The class 5 4–6–0 as built	52
19	No. 73030 leaves Nottingham with a St Pancras express	53
20	A class 5 4–6–0 acts as pilot through Monessie Gorge	54
21	BR standard class 5MT 4–6–0 no. 73115, 'King Pellinore'	55
22	One of the class 5s no. 73031 pauses at Sheffield Midland	56
23	No. 73157 with a down 'Cambridge Buffet Express'	57
24	No. 73010 crossing the Midland main line at Loughborough	58
25	A class 5 4–6–0 fitted with Caprotti valve gear	59
26	Scene on the WR's Cambrian line	60

27 No. 75028 assisting a 'Castle' 4–6–0 up Dainton bank 61
28 A standard class 4 4–6–0 62
29 No. 75029 assisting a 'West Country' Pacific 63
30 An SR-based class 4 4–6–0 with the flush-sided BR1B tender 64
31 No. 76001 leaving Mallaig 65
32 Ayr-based no. 76097 with a Kilmarnock local 66
33 One of Leicester Midland's class 4 2–6–0s 67
34 A standard class 4 locomotive at Albury 70
35 A class 3 2–6–0 pilots an Ivatt class 4 into Tebay 71
36 No. 77014 mounts Upwey bank 72
37 One of the Millhouse shed's class 2 2–6–0s 73
38 No. 78007 accelerating away from Barmouth 74
39 A class 4 2–6–4T heading for Watford Tunnel 77
40 Double-heading a special past Upper Port Glasgow 78
41 SR class 4 2–6–4T no. 80032 on the Cuckoo Line 79
42 No. 80097 leaving Southend Central 80
43 The down 'Harrogate Sunday Pullman' near Weeton 81
44 An exiled class 4 2–6–4T on the Cambrian line 82
45 No. 80147 helps no. 35011, 'General Steam Navigation' 83
46 4.25 pm Exeter Central–Exmouth leaving Woodbury Road 84
47 No. 82009 heads a Barmouth–Dovey Junction train 85
48 SR class 3 2–6–2T no. 82017 heading the 'Bournemouth Belle' 86
49 Auto-fitted class 2 2–6–2T no. 84007 87
50 Class 9 2–10–0 no. 92013 on the test plant at Rugby 90
51 No. 92140 passing through Hadley Wood Station 91
52 A class 9 2–10–0 on the Tyne Dock–Consett iron ore haul 92
53 An Annesley–Woodford 'Windcutter' on the GC main line 93
54 No. 92069 on the up 'South Yorkshireman' 94
55 Crosti 2–10–0 under construction 96
56 No. 92025 blanketing its cab with exhaust 97
57 A Crosti rebuilt as an orthodox steam locomotive 99
58 Double-chimney class 9 2–10–0 no. 92223 with BR1G tender 100
59 The sole Giesl-ejector-fitted 2–10–0, no. 92250 103
60 Last of the line 104

Author's Preface

The concept of a British standard steam locomotive range was only the first of the post-war succession of changes which numerous Jeremiahs prophesied would kill off British railway enthusiasm. I can remember deep suspicion of regular-interval passenger timetables, let alone of dieselisation and electrification. But thirty years on, railway enthusiasm is at a new peak. And the BR standard steam types, despite the probability that only two of them consistently outclassed the work of pre-1948 designs which they superseded, excite as much nostalgic interest as any breed in British locomotive history.

That on its own would scarcely justify another book on BR standard steam. No group of classes in history had its rationale, its design detail, successive modifications and even its performance on test so thoroughly documented in its lifetime, let alone in retrospect. One criticism at least could never be levelled at the locomotive engineers of the BTC's Railway Executive, that they were secretive about the shortcomings of their steam products: these were as frankly disclosed in the published bulletins on the testing of each class as the redoubtable feats of the Britannia Pacifics

The gap that this book chiefly attempts to fill is that of operational career history. I have summarised the main features of each design as a preliminary to each chapter, but for the most part have traced the areas of work to which the different batches of each type were assigned, then progressively reassigned as they were ousted by dieselisation or electrification.

Blockley, Glos
April 1981

G. FREEMAN ALLEN

I
Genesis

British Railways was born with a desperate need of new locomotives. Looking back from the early 1980s, when BR's annual additions to stock of new locomotives and power cars barely top three figures, it is surprising to find that the 600 locomotives a year, which the Attlee Government's Minister of Economic Affairs, Sir Stafford Cripps, promised the railways steel enough to build in the crisis-wracked year of 1947, were regarded as dangerously short commons. The difference between then and now is, in large measure, a reflection of BR's subsequent contraction and the superior availability for work of diesel and electric traction. But the 1947 provision also underlines the limited construction of new power during the Second World War, the number and diversity of over-aged machines which BR consequently inherited, and the near exhaustion to which much of the fleet had been driven, by a combination of skimped maintenance and ruthless flogging.

The government was emphatic that the country's sickly economy could not cope with main line electrification, though Lord President of the Council Herbert Morrison, excoriating the 'Big Four' for failure to act on the 1925 Weir Report's advocacy of total main line electrification alongside establishment of the national grid, had promised during the Commons debate on the 1947 Transport Bill that 'in the public ownership scheme which we envisage, capital – and cheap capital – will be available for electrification as soon as it becomes practicable and expedient'. (The Weir report, incidentally, reckoned that the whole system, bar lightly trafficked branches could have been electrified over two decades or so for a cost at 1925 prices of £241 million.)

Inability to electrify determined Robin A. Riddles, the former LMS engineer, then wartime head of the Ministry of Supply's Transportation Materials Directorate, and finally LMS Vice-President who was appointed the Railway Executive's Member for mechanical affairs, to persist with steam. If capital cost was the all-important criterion, his was certainly the only course. In the state of diesel traction art at the time, with no standard models to take straight from British industry's shelf, the first cost of a 1,600 hp diesel was likely to quintuple that of a steam class 5 4–6–0; the price ratio per pound of tractive effort would still disfavour the diesel by as much as three to one. Nevertheless, some of Riddles' superiors had misgivings.

In the spring of 1948 BTC Chairman Sir Cyril (later Lord) Hurcomb asked that the Railway Executive appoint a non-engineering committee to look into the economic rather than the well-worn technical arguments for the different forms of traction. Impressed by a study of diesel locomotive operation in the USA and of railcars in Europe, their report implied that Riddles' policy was only improving the pavement of a blind alley; there should be a substantial investment in diesel shunters, a purposeful study of a diesel multiple-unit fleet's potential, and an experiment with 2,000 hp diesels. But their report did not materialise until 1951 when the standard steam locomotive programme was well under way. That was the year the Railway Executive's first Chairman, Sir Eustace Missenden, retired, but not before he too had hinted in remarks to the Institute of Transport that he would have preferred a diesel traction transition to the first choice of electrification. To that, however, Riddles was firmly opposed, partly in the belief that diesel traction would prove so costly as to starve the railways of money for electrification. It was claimed, too, that most BR operating men were too set in their steam ways to fancy adaptation to a new form of power – and certainly the treatment both of the five main line prototypes inherited from the LMS and SR, even that of the 1955 'pilot scheme' diesels on at least one Region, lent the allegation credence.

So the LNER's post-war plan to order twenty-five main line diesel locomotives for the East Coast route and eighty railcars for trial throughout its system as a first step in dieselisation was dismissed to the archives and the Riddles team set about formulating its steam construction programme. Since the BTC had deliberately centralised the design of locomotives and rolling stock, and the prescriptions for their maintenance and operation with the Railway Executive, type standardisation for future construction was inevitable. However, because the need of new locomotives was imperative and would not brook delay while new designs were formulated, the Regions were permitted to construct a further 1,538 locomotives to existing designs between 1948 and 1951. One of the Regional Chief Mechanical Engineers (now stripped of so much of their authority to originate design by the new order) mounted a particularly vigorous campaign for the retention of Regional designs ad infinitum, but he was baying politically – as well as technically – for the moon.

In the interests of economy in operation, construction and upkeep all four pre-1948 companies had set a locomotive standardisation course, though the LNER and SR did so well after the GWR and LMS, and one of these ranges might have been picked for BR if it met the essential qualification of all-line route availability. On that count only the LMS types were eligible. But although Riddles had chosen two LMS alumni to sit on his left and right hand – R. C. Bond as Chief Officer (Locomotive Construction and Maintenance) and E. S. Cox as Executive Officer (Design) – both of whom he had worked with in his LMS days in the 1930s, he sagely ordered a rigorous comparative examination of pre-1948 designs in the principal express passenger, mixed traffic and heavy freight categories as a prologue to the detailed formulation of a new building programme. As a further safeguard against any accusation of unwarranted bias he also insisted that not only the tests themselves but the finest print of their findings be publicised to laymen as well as railwaymen.

The ensuing Locomotive Exchanges of the summer of 1948 were inconclusive for any of the types examined, partly because the Regional enginemen that went from route to route with their locomotives approached the trials with differing attitudes of mind – the contrast between the élan of the SR Pacific drivers and the conservatism of the LMR men was particularly sharp. Sparkling efforts by the Gresley A4 Pacific and the Bulleid light Pacific lost lustre because of the former's hot middle big-end flushes and the latter's extravagant habits. One incontrovertible conclusion did emerge, however: that it was possible to embody in a single type not only all-purpose capability from 90 mph, medium-weight express passenger haulage to economical freight and stopping passenger duty, but also compatibility with all but branch line route availability from Cornwall to Caithness.

It is worth noting here that an additional exchange was mooted which would have been enthralling. In 1950, with time to spare before construction of more express passenger Pacifics was warranted, Bond proposed that more data on the relative merits and maintenance costs of three as opposed to four cylinders be assembled to underpin a decision on the prospective BR class 8 4–6–2 by exchanging five Stanier Duchess and five Peppercorn class A1 Pacifics between King's Cross and Camden sheds for an extended period. Disappointingly for the enthusiast the suggestion was not taken up.

Throughout the first five months of 1948 Riddles had had a Locomotive Standards Committee (to the chair of which he astutely appointed a Swindon man, A. W. J. Dymond) digging into the economic and technical records of representative pre-1948 mixed traffic types in different power categories, and running the rule over how far they satisfied the civil engineers. The principal objective was to establish which pre-1948 types were best left in production pending the completion of new designs, but the committee produced a double-edged report that on the one hand found none of the twenty-two types it examined so markedly superior as to win it the vote above the rest, and on the other set out such a gloomy list of the costs and inconveniences of inflicting 'foreign' types on motive power depots and workshops that it implicitly damned the creation of a new standard range of classes.

Riddles, however, was not to be deflected from the decision he had taken after his appointment to the Railway Executive in 1947 to breed a new range of locomotives. The various tests and analyses of the first half of 1948 would only help to crystallise the requirements and emphasise the features of pre-1948 design that were worth incorporating in the new types to come. That was also to be inferred by E. S. Cox's completion as early as June 1948 – only a fortnight after the Locomotive Standards Committee had pronounced, and while the Locomotive Exchanges were still in progress – of an outline programme of twelve types for construction. Four of these – two class 7 4–6–2s, one specifically express passenger, the other mixed traffic, a class 6 4–6–2 and a class 9 2–8–2 – were advocated as brand new designs. Three were proposed as substantial reworkings of existing types: these were a class 8 4–6–2, class 4 4–6–0 and class 3 2–6–2 tank. The remaining class 4 2–6–0, class 4 2–6–4 tank and class 2 2–6–0 and 2–6–2 tank were recommended as detail revisions of existing designs.

One did not have to be a clairvoyant to deduce the 'existing types' in mind. In the nature of things the inspiration of the standard locomotive range was bound to be LMS, since Riddles and his two top aides had been schooled in LMS practice. That apart, however, the LMS under Stanier and his successors had made design for universal route availability a keystone of its traction policy, and this chimed with the nationalised system's need more harmoniously than any other company's practice. The other keynote of LMS policy was even more relevant to the conditions in which the nationalised system opened its account: that was its concern in the last pre-war years to design for increased mileage between overhauls and for less labour-intensive maintenance, through the incorporation of self-cleaning smokeboxes, rocking grates, self-emptying ashpans, and so on. In other features the LMS under Stanier and afterwards had arguably produced the simplest and most economical mixed traffic locomotives in Europe.

Cox had been careful to propound entirely new designs only where innovation promised a gain in technical efficiency or operational flexibility over the potential of existing types. That was clearly the case with the class 7 4–6–2s. The available motive power stock offered nothing compatible with Great Eastern axle-loading and dimensional limitations that had the power (or for that matter the ease of maintenance) to realise the accelerated fixed-interval timetable the ER had boldly drafted for the Liverpool Street–Ipswich–Norwich route. This ER enterprise was indirectly a blessing for the ex-LMS Royal Scots. Had it not generated a nicely timed and economically acceptable demand for additions to BR's overall class 7 steam strength, the Riddles' team contemplated making room for their new type by halting the taper-boiler reconstruction of Fowler's original parallel-boiler 4–6–0s and scrapping the residue of unconverted engines.

Subsequent chapters recount how mature consideration refined this outline scheme to the twelve classes totalling 999 locomotives that were ultimately built. All the eventual designs, however, were characterised by the basic principles which Riddles and his team had agreed from the start.

Simplicity was to be the keynote, to help make the engines resilient to the unsophisticated handling and common-user rough-and-tumble prevalent on the post-war railway. Largely on that account two cylinders would be the standard arrangement almost throughout the range, but other persuasive grounds for this decision were reduced first cost, elimination of fallible mechanism and the belief that a four-beats-per-wheel-revolution exhaust was conducive to better steaming. Boilers would be the biggest consistent with the axle-load and loading gauge parameters set for each type, to maximise steam generation capacity; so would firegrate areas, with the aim of controlling combustion at economical levels when the engines were not being pressed; and the engines would have modern long-lap valve gear and high temperature superheating.

Another important goal was the attainment of high adhesion factors, which amongst other things dictated adoption of a multi-valve regulator combined with the superheater header – a device some doubted had the extra sensitivity of control to justify its greater expense. In the event adhesion was one quality wherein the standard Pacifics, the class 6 Clans especially, did not in practice match specification; the Riddles team realised too late how much the up-grade assurance of the Pacific protagonists in the 1948 Exchanges derived from the artistry of the senior drivers which each Region had specially picked to travel with them. That was the case above all with the Bulleid light Pacifics from the SR, the versatility of which had been the mainspring of the BR class 6 proposal.

The new engines had to be easy and cheap to service. That predicated all the aids to simpler shed routines built into the most recent LMS types, such as self-cleaning smokeboxes, rocking grates and self-emptying ashpans, more recourse to mechanical and grease lubrication, and acceptance of the increased cost of manganese steel liners for axle-box bearings and horn blocks. These liners had in recent LMS experience done as much if not more to prolong mileage between workshop retirements as roller bearings. Finally, the new locomotives were to be made simpler and more comfortable to drive by an ergonomic redesign of the traditional British engine cab, its layout and its fittings.

The new regime had retained the chief drawing offices of the pre-1948 'Big Four', at Brighton, Derby, Doncaster and Swindon, and the detail development of the standard types was distributed between them. However, Cox held the reins on behalf of Riddles, so that the Regional CMEs had to resign themselves to a kibitzer's rôle as their staff drew to direction from London; by all accounts the Regional chiefs bore it without public rancour, give or take a piquant aside as they toured their drawing offices and glanced over shoulders. Each drawing office was allocated the parental responsibility for working up one or more of the standard types, but in addition they were variously assigned the preparation of standard components for the whole range: Brighton for the brakes and sanding gear; Derby for bogies, wheels, tyres, axles, springs and tenders; Doncaster for coupling and connecting rods, cylinder and valve gear detail; and Swindon for steam parts, boiler and smokebox detail.

Choice of a colour scheme for the nationalised system had been deliberated eagerly by the national as well as the railway press in the closing weeks of 1947. Many half-expected the Attlee Government to nudge the BTC into adoption of Post Office red, but the BTC was left to exercise its own opinion. Riddles was set on black, to his mind the only sensible hue for such an inherently dirty machine as the steam locomotive, and an economical one because it was the most durable, and also the one that could be touched up without the worry that repainted and unrepainted areas would not match. The post-war shortage of shed cleaners reinforced his argument, but the BTC was not persuaded. On the other hand, it does not seem to have offered any firm alternatives of its own.

Consequently the three Stanier class 5 4–6–0s, which were then repainted to model other styles before the full might of the BTC and Railway Executive at what is now Kensington Olympia on 30 January 1948, all paraded known liveries – no. 4762 Southern, malachite green; no. 4763 LNER, apple green; and no. 4764, GWR Brunswick green. Also on hand was SR electric locomotive no. CC2 in an approximation of the onetime Caledonian Railway pale blue, with silver lining. None of these won full-throated approved, so Riddles signalled to the wings of a nearby siding where he had concealed his own choice. Out steamed no. 5292, needless to say in the former LNWR lined black. And lined black all standard types became apart from the Pacifics (and a number of humbler types passing through Swindon works during the 'Great Western Region' heyday of the 1960s), which qualified for the subsequent lined Brunswick green livery applied to all but principal express passenger locomotives. For these last a lined royal blue livery was reserved in the early years of nationalisation, but eventually they too were Brunswick green.

2
The Class 7 Pacifics

No. 70000, the first two-cylinder Pacific to operate in Britain, emerged from Crewe works at the start of 1951. After a few weeks of running-in on public service trains between Crewe and Carlisle she headed south for her ceremonial naming as 'Britannia' by the Minister of Transport, Alfred Barnes, before a phalanx of British Transport Commission mandarins, BR officers and press at Marylebone station on 30 January. That naming ceremony, incidentally, was the last public duty as BTC Chairman of Sir Eustace Missenden, who was succeeded next day by the subsequently knighted John Elliot.

There was scarcely a layman that day who was unsurprised at 'Britannia's' two-cylinder layout. The received wisdom of the previous twenty years or more was that one advisedly employed three or four cylinders to minimise high-speed hammer-blow on the track without heavily weighting balance of the reciprocating machinery. But in BR's new class 7, it was claimed, hammer-blow had been limited to half the force regarded as the limit of tolerance by lightening the valve motion parts. With the hammer-blow objection overcome, two-cylinder propulsion had a great deal going for it: reduced first cost, a cut of some 3½ tons in weight and simplicity and ease of accessibility for maintenance (a cylinder more, it was said, and the engine would take at least a third as much time to prepare for a day's work).

Since the newcomer was billed as a mixed traffic type, intended to have the versatility of a Gresley V2 2–6–2 as well as the express passenger dash of a Swindon Castle or an LM Royal Scot, its 6 ft 2 in. driving wheels were a logical choice. The wide range of work in mind for the Pacific also dictated a single rather than a double chimney and blastpipe. Studies conducted on the stationary test rigs then operational at Swindon works and at the recently opened BR locomotive test plant at Rugby suggested that devices calculated to create more smokebox vacuum for a specific back pressure could be a drawback when the engine was on a light rein.

But the new Pacifics were frequently driven hard, and at up to 90 mph. In the final decades of BR steam every pre-nationalisation class in the same league of inter-city passenger work had at least some of its members modified with a double blastpipe and chimney, yet one never heard any clamour for retrospective alteration of the Britannias.

That seems commentary enough on the free-steaming characteristics of the original design, and on the aim to obtain them with any type of coal. The boiler featured 5½ in. diameter flue tubes – the most ample ever used in Britain – to secure a higher measure of superheating, and

Cecil J Allen Collection

1. As built – no. 70001, 'Lord Hurcomb', one of the first batch of class 7 4–6–2s which started their career on the Eastern Region's Great Eastern Line.

that blessed the Britannia with a free gas area between firebox and smokebox which was inferior only to the space in a Stanier Duchess boiler, so far as British locomotives were concerned. Wide passages eased the steam flow to the two 20 in. by 28 in. cylinders, in which 11 in. diameter piston valves and 2¼ in. wide piston valves assured high output. Significant, too, was the design of the steam chests so that the volume between valve heads was half that of the pistons' swept volume within the cylinders.

There was no startling innovation in 'Britannia' as a steam traction unit, just a closely-reasoned mix of known technology. The one item quite new in British practice was the rearward extension of the cab over the front of the tender, which did away with the unsteady fall-plate link between the two and allowed the fireman to do all his work on the cab floor. The improved working environment of post-war industrial plants was already highlighting the discomforts of life with steam traction, and the Railway Executive had done all it could think of to mitigate them in the standard cab design. Not only that, but it had summoned delegations of locomotive men at all levels to run the rule over a full-scale mock-up at its London headquarters.

This consultation generally approved the regrouping of the controls for easy reach by a seated driver and his fireman, the improved

2. Debut on the Great Eastern Line – the 'Norfolkman', one of the trains selected to premiere the new BR standard crimson and cream livery in Festival of Britain year, threads Belstead Cutting near Ipswich en route for Norwich behind class 7 4–6–2 no. 70003, 'John Bunyan', on 21 May 1951.

P M Alexander/Colourviews Ltd

look-out both ways, the way hot piping had been cut short on the firebox sides and kept out of the cab, along with several other refinements. Had the viewing been staged in a wind tunnel more than one participant would have realised that the gap between overhanging cab and tender sucked in a vicious gale that was the more uncomfortable because the boiler front was no longer draped with steam-filled pipes. That had to be countered after the first engines were in service by adding a tender fallplate and plugging the side gaps with crude-looking canvas screens, which were later replaced by more seemly rubber fairings. After that some drivers complained they were too hot, a complaint remedied by extra pipe lagging.

Cecil J Allen Collection

3. A celebrated pairing – Stewarts Lane shed's class 7 4–6–2 no. 70004, 'William Shakespeare', and the SR 'Golden Arrow', pulling out of Victoria on 6 June 1952.

Scenting a type with the power to effect a significant acceleration of its Great Eastern expresses, and with the dimensions and axle weights to satisfy that line's stringent civil engineering restrictions – essential matching qualifications that even Gresley had not met – the Eastern Region had lodged a claim to the first class 7 Pacifics as soon as their outline specification was known. It was not only 'Britannia's' physique that appealed to them. The ER planned, for the first time in Britain, to apply to a locomotive-hauled inter-city service the principles of intensive, regular-interval timetabling with fixed formation train-sets previously conceivable only with electric multiple units. For that it needed simple, easy-to-maintain machines; and here again the prospective Pacific design, with its simple layout, rocking grate, self-emptying ashpan, self-cleaning smokebox and roller bearing axle-boxes throughout, filled the bill.

To prove that the schedules they were drafting were not unrealistic for a Pacific of the BR class 7's estimated power, the ER borrowed Southern Battle of Britain 4–6–2 no. 34059, 'Sir Archibald Sinclair', during May 1949 and set it successfully to some of the timings in mind. So the first fifteen of the new engines were earmarked for the Great Eastern, though there was an agonising phase when the ER, its timetable plan complete almost to the last footnote, had to contend with Railway Executive misgivings that these standard bearers of a unitary motive power policy deserved a more up-market showcase than bucolic East Anglia. At the end of the

Brian Morrison

4. Of the three class 7 4–6–2s from the first batch which were subtracted from the ER allocation for duty on the SR, no. 70009, 'Alfred the Great', was at first allocated to Nine Elms shed and for a period was entrusted with the 'Bournemouth Belle', here passing Clapham Junction on 23 June 1951.

bout the ER did have to surrender three of its putative allocation, nos. 70004, 70009 and 70014, to the Southern in exchange for a trio of Bulleid light Pacifics, nos. 34039, 34057 and 34065, which arrived at Stratford in the spring of 1951.

No. 70000 went straight from the Marylebone naming to Liverpool Street–Norwich service from Stratford depot – and on its second up trip, on the wet Sunday night of 2 February, strewed its right-hand piston head and cylinder cover over the track at Marks Tey. That was put right with spares rushed from the production line at Crewe, but twelve days later the engine's other piston head disintegrated; a few days more and fresh cylinder parts were breaking up in the same way. The bother was soon traced to an unforeseen liability to malfunction of the steam drier arrangement in the multiple-valve regulator, which in certain working conditions admitted considerable quantities of water to the cylinders. Modification sorted out the difficulty before many of the Pacifics had been commissioned.

Britannia no. 70005, 'John Milton', was submitted to the Railway Executive's locomotive efficiency testing routine almost straight from the assembly line at Crewe. It had run only 560 miles when in April 1951 it was handed over to the Rugby Test Plant, where a press party was invited the following month to watch it pounding vainly away on the rollers. To take us down from Euston to Rugby the newest Britannia of the hour, no. 70009, 'Alfred the Great', was mobilised and attached, along with the LM dynamometer car, to the 10.30 am to Liverpool. Permanent way work inhibited the engine going down, but on the return when Pacific and the three-car press section were coupled on to the 1.55 pm Wolverhampton–Euston the civil engineer was much kinder.

'Alfred the Great' had dubious coal to master as well as fourteen coaches grossing 470 tons, with the result that boiler pressure was 60 lb off the full 250 lb rating at Tring summit, but that did not seem to throttle back its steam-making. The driver simply widened the cut-off to 35 per cent and topped the bank at 62.5 mph in the course of a sparkling performance that had more than recovered 9 minutes of a late start from Rugby, and shaved a minute off the pre-war 'Coronation Scot' booking of 49 minutes for the 57.4 miles from Blisworth to Willesden. To excel pre-war standards in 1951 was as rare an experience as a single-figure wage claim in 1981.

Back on the rollers at Rugby, then on the usual open road testing ground of the steeply graded trans-Pennine main line between Skipton and Carlisle, no. 70005 and later no. 70025 were compiling a dossier of performance which, by the conclusion of the programme in February 1953, would yield much more impressive testimony to the Britannia's steaming capacity. To probe capability to the limit, two firemen were employed during these routines. That way the Pacifics could be fired at an average rate of 2½ tons an hour, which at one stage of no. 70005's examination on the road had her generating steam at the phenomenal level of 37,560 lb/hr. At the head of a load equivalent to 850 tons – the actual train weight was increased to this figure by use of the dynamic braking apparatus in the mobile test cars it included – no. 70005 negotiated the 22.85 miles southbound from Lazonby to Crosby Garrett, which gradually steepen to 1 in 100/162 for much of the final 10 miles, in 29.25 minutes. Most of the way the Pacific was on full regulator and 40–45 per cent cut-off, but on the steepest pitches the driver gave her as much as 55 per cent without the engine losing her feet.

It is a pity stereophonic tape recording was not the commonplace in 1951 that it is today. However majestically the exhaust of no. 70005 rang around the hillsides on that Carlisle–Skipton run, the effect cannot have been half as stunning as the ear-splitting tattoo it beat on the walls of the Rugby Test Plant. During our visit they had the braking of the rollers adjusted to simulate the resistance of a 500 ton load on a 1 in 90 slope, against which no. 70005 was battling at a steady 25 mph on full regulator and 40 per cent cut-off. Neither visually nor aurally has my railway reporting life since come up with anything as awesome.

The transformed GE Liverpool Street–Norwich timetable was launched with the 1951 summer timetable, which that year did not start until 2 July because BR was desperate for train crews to clear a chaotic backlog of freight traffic. Each way the train service was reorganised on a fixed-interval departure basis, on the half-hour from London and at 45 minutes past from Norwich, with the fastest trains in each direction set unprecedented overall schedules of 2 hours 10 minutes on restricted nine-coach loads of 300 tons maximum. The 5.30 pm down, calling at Chelmsford, Ipswich, Stowmarket and Diss, but even so allowed only 2 hours 26 minutes to Norwich, was as much as 46 minutes faster than its counterpart in the preceding timetable, the 5.08 pm.

To operate the new schedules Norwich and Stratford shared ten Pacifics. The rosters included double return trips daily for four engines, and where these diagrams included a

Cecil J Allen Collection

5. In the 1950s the LMR's class 7 4–6–2s were based at Manchester's Longsight shed and were regular performers on Euston expresses: no. 70043, accelerating past Kilburn with the 2.40 pm from Euston, was one of the two class 7s sent into service deflector-less, unnamed, and dual-braked with a pair of Westinghouse pumps for Midland line trials of prototype air and vacuum-fitted coal wagon sets.

turn via Ely, the Pacific involved was chalking up a mileage of more than 2,800 in the week. That was a remarkable aggregate for a British steam locomotive shuttling between cities less than 150 miles apart.

The stage had been set for the GE Britannias by some remedial track work, and before long the Diss dip had become one of the likeliest spots on BR to clock 90 mph in the early 1950s. Perhaps more impressive was the Pacifics' pace on the level and the way they could scale the 1 in 103 of Brentwood bank at 50 mph. 'What might have appeared an extremely hard booking of 11 minutes for the 10.2 miles from Chadwell Heath to Shenfield,' wrote an astonished Cecil J. Allen, 'turns out to be a perfectly simple proposition.' An old GE man himself, he could not resist underlining that the ten principal GE weekday expresses were now more tightly timed over their East Anglian switchback than the ten best over the Western's comparative billiard table between Paddington and Bristol.

In the autumn of 1952 the Britannias were set a 2 hour London–Norwich timing inclusive of an Ipswich stop, with the down afternoon 'Broadsman'. It remained unique until the allowance was standardised – with the addition of a Colchester stop – in the route's fully dieselised schedules of the 1962 summer. It was with the 'Broadsman' that probably the fastest run of all GE line steam history was notched, when no. 70035 dismissed the 46.3 sharply undulating miles from Ipswich to Norwich in just over 39 minutes start to stop, averaging 84.4 mph for 26.5 miles, and touching 94 mph in the Diss dip.

GE enginemen's respect for the Britannias was almost total. Compared with their B1, B12 and B17 4–6–0s of the day before they found the Pacifics' power 'almost frightening when it was applied with vigour', to quote Stratford's well-known shedmaster of the 1950s, Richard Hardy. Most had learned their craft under an illustrious LNER steam operator of earlier years, L. P. Parker, who preached use of full regulator wherever possible and variation of cut-off to get the maximum productivity from steam by expansion. That was just the technique to get the best from a Britannia, which thus driven could keep the fastest GE point-to-point times over the route's easier stretches on only 10–12 per cent cut-off.

Most of the GE Britannias were individually allocated to specific sets of crews in the 1950s and that, coupled with as keen a concern among fitters as well as enginemen to make the best of the engines, was a vital factor in the Pacifics' consistent performance. To cite Richard Hardy once more, writing in the mid-1950s: 'When the time comes to propose a Britannia for general or intermediate repair, it is difficult to find sufficient evidence on which to base a report mechanically. Admittedly, tube leakage begins to assert itself when the higher mileages are achieved, but the normal mechanical ailments which help to get an engine to the shops never show themselves.'

One more serious mechanical weakness did need eradicating before the Pacifics got into their stride, however. Throughout the summer of 1951 no. 70004, 'William Shakespeare', had been one of the full-size railway exhibits on a staging at the extravagant Festival of Britain on London's South Bank site. Released at the end of September, it was refurbished at the SR's Eastleigh works and then, on 11 October, applied to the accelerated 'Golden Arrow' as a crowning touch to the re-equipment of this train with a new Pullman rake earlier in the year. The Chairman and the full strength of his Railway Executive paraded at Victoria station to see no. 70004 off, but within ten days they were knitting brows over an alarming incident to the train. Making considerable speed near Headcorn, the Pacific snapped a connecting rod.

So potentially disastrous a failure on a train as prestigious as the 'Arrow' naturally roused the shock-horror probers of Fleet Street, and it emerged that this was the seventh in a succession of instances of Britannia driving wheels shifting on their axles, the first of which had befallen no. 70014 back in July. The Railway Executive decided that something was endemically wrong and ordered all Britannias immobilised for a diagnosis, which soon fixed the cause as a combination of detail in the fitting of the roller bearings to the driving axles. The side-tracking of the Britannias for preventive action inevitably dislocated GE operations for a couple of months, though the Railway Executive did hand Stratford a couple more Bulleid light Pacifics from the SR, nos. 34076 and 34089, and two new BR standard class 5 4–6–0s, nos. 73000 and 73002, as temporary makeweights. (All five SR Pacifics, incidentally, were returned to their native heath between December 1951 and May 1952; during their sojourn on the GE

6. On the Western in June 1958 class 7 4–6–2 no. 70025, 'Western Star', has its deflector handrails removed and replaced by handholds, a move to improve the crew's view of signals following the Milton accident; also visible are the rubber bellows inserted between cab and tender to counteract footplate draughts. No. 70025's tender is the BR1A, with increased 5,000 gallon water capacity. The scene is Newport (Mon.), the train is the 7.50 am Paddington–Fishguard.

G F Heiron

line they were scarcely ever used on the fastest schedules.)

While the SR was acquiring its first Britannias for Victoria–Dover/Folkestone boat train duty, the London Midland too was allocated a sample pair. No. 70015 was sent to Camden in July and deputed to the 8.30 am Euston–Liverpool and the 5.25 pm 'Red Rose' back, while no. 70016 was posted to Leeds Holbeck, which employed it both northwards over Ais Gill summit to Carlisle and to London, where this Pacific made its debut with the up 'Thames–Clyde Express' on 7 August 1951. But the next recipient of Britannias en masse was the Western.

The residue of the first batch of twenty-five Pacifics, nos. 70017–24, was shared initially between the Western's Old Oak and Laira depots, from the former to cover chiefly Paddington–Bristol workings, from the latter work west of Newton Abbot. At both ends of the line, but more especially in the far West, they were as welcome as an English try at Cardiff Arms Park.

Politically, the influx of standard designs could not have been worse timed. The country was on the brink of the October 1951 General Election, for which the political platform of Churchill's Tories included a pledge to emasculate the BTC's Railway Executive. In spirit the land west of Paddington was still the Great Western. If the Tories won they seemed certain to make it more or less the Great Western again *de jure* and *de facto* (in the event, they did not, of course). So why inflict these heathen machines on the WR – and the indignity was compounded by the blasphemy of naming them after some of Swindon's lustrous products of the past – just when providence looked likely to lift the detested yoke of London Midland-based standardisation? The Railway Executive's public relations apparatus, one should add, had irritated Western men still more by its tendency to portray the Britannias as the apotheosis of British steam technology in general, not just of simple, trouble-free design for general purpose work. That invited scornful comparison with Swindon's Kings, let alone Castles.

What Stratford men had made of the Britannias was irrelevant. To the vast majority of Western enginemen there was only one way to lay out an engine cab and one driving doctrine. In both cases they were Swindon's and in neither did the Britannias conform. Not surprisingly the initial work of the WR Pacifics was drab.

Light began to glimmer after the allocation to Cardiff Canton of the next five Pacifics, nos. 70025–9, in the autumn of 1952. This quintet was equipped with the Type BR1A tender, with 5,000 gallons water capacity instead of the 4,250 gallons of the first twenty-five Pacifics' BR1; the coal capacity of 7 tons was the same for each type.

At the South Wales depot the Western Britannias came under the control of men who were prepared to accept that it needed unaccustomed technique to make the best of them. Throughout the Pacifics' career on the WR the South Wales–London steam schedules were never demanding, granted, but by the later 1950s the Canton engines were comfortably master with loads of 400 tons plus. Rationalisation of spares distribution was the main reason, but Canton's way with the Pacifics was undoubtedly some motivation for concentration of all WR Britannias on that depot at the start of 1957. It was cleared of Castle 4–6–0s to make room for them. Bitching about the Pacifics remained so chronic, though, that in July the BR mechanical chief, Robin Riddles, and his aides were stung into parading the whole brigade of senior WR locomotive inspectors at their headquarters for what diplomatic communique draftsmen would euphemise as a frank exchange of views. Pinned down, the WR men could adduce little but hard-riding, draughty cabs, and an inbred disaffection for anything but Swindon design of engine and controls, as justification for their mistrust of the Pacifics.

The unfamiliar left-hand driving position of the Britannia cab was a repeated grievance, especially as so many ex-GW semaphore signals were sited for best view from the right-hand side of the cab, and it was underlined by the one train accident with passenger fatalities to befall a Britannia. Oblivious to the warning of the diversion for track work in his weekly notice, bothered by bad weather, a refractory injector, and with a fireman who did not know the route too well, the driver of no. 70026 on a Sunday Treherbert–Paddington excursion not only missed sight of signals routeing him from up fast to slow at Milton box, between Steventon and Didcot, but allegedly ignored and cancelled the AWS warning of a cautionary aspect. So his

7. Class 7 4–6–2 no. 70045, 'Lord Rowallan', was one of the last ten Britannias built with flush-sided BR1D tenders of 4,725 gallon and 9 tons' capacity, and fitted with steam-powered coal pushers. Externally disreputable, no. 70045 was photographed in the late 1950s spell of Britannia duty on the Midland main line, hauling the up 'Waverley' south of Nottingham near Widmerpool.

T G Hepburn/Rail Archive Stephenson

train hit the crossover at about 50 mph, derailed catastrophically, and killed eleven of its passengers. One outcome of the subsequent inquiry was that the Western Britannias' smoke deflectors were stripped of their vertical handrails and had handholds cut into them instead, as some effort to reduce interference with the driver's view ahead.

With the batch of Britannias delivered during 1953, nos. 70030–44, the tenders were again the small BR1 type. That was a misjudgement so far as the first five were concerned. They were assigned to the LMR, which had booked them for Holyhead. Within a few days no. 70030's appetite for coal on the through 'Irish Mail' run to Euston was found to outrun the tender's capacity and the quintet was quickly reallocated to Manchester's Longsight depot. Nos. 70035–52 swelled the GE studs at Stratford and Norwich to accommodate the summer 1953 extension of accelerated, regular-interval timetabling to the Cambridge route between Liverpool Street and Norwich – a revolution which, incidentally, gave Cambridge a fastest ever non-stop schedule of 64 minutes to London by the Sunday 7.15 pm.

8. Displaced by dieselisation of the GE main line, some Britannia Pacifics were in 1961 assigned to Immingham for Cleethorpes–King's Cross express duty: one of them, no. 70041, 'Sir John Moore', tops Potters Bar summit with the 6.50 pm from King's Cross that year.

Brian Stephenson

The last two of this batch, nos. 70043/4, were outshopped without smoke deflectors because their space was needed for frame-mounted Westinghouse pumps. Because of this they were also unnamed at first, though that deficiency was rectified when the pumps were removed after they had served their purpose. The reason was a series of high-speed trials with specially-prepared rakes of continuously braked coal wagons, which were conducted on the Midland main line between Toton and Brent over a number of Sundays to provide data for a decision on future freight wagon braking practice. Between tests the two Pacifics concerned were appropriated for some Midland as well as Western Division express passenger work in 1954.

In the second half of 1954 Holyhead did get Britannias that matched its job specification, as the final series, nos. 70045–54, were turned out with the Type BR1D standard tender, which had room for 9 tons of coal. Of these nos. 70045–9 went to the LM shed, while the remainder were the first of the class to be based in Scotland, at Glasgow Polmadie, which slotted the newcomers into its class 7P rosters both to Perth and Aberdeen. A feature of this final ten was some modification of the cab structure in a fresh effort to mute the whining at its draughtiness. Bereft of inspiration, inclination, or both, the BR headquarters sent all ten into the world nameless. The Scots started to name their quintet early in 1955, but the LMR kept its five

9. Work from Immingham breaks more new ground for a Britannia: on 27 April 1962 no. 70035, 'Rudyard Kipling', takes the ex-LDEC route near Mansfield with the Grimsby–Whitland fish train.

J Cupit

anonymous until the end of the decade – and even then ran out of ideas after four had been titled, sending no. 70047 nameless to its grave.

From the start Riddles and his team had been dubious of the virtue of roller bearings on all driving axles, especially as under Stanier and Ivatt the London Midland had done a great deal to perfect reliable, wear-resistant plain bearings. When it came to nos. 70035–9 the BR men decided to put the issue to the test by confining roller bearings to the centre driving axle; then in nos. 70040–9 they employed plain bearings for all driving axles. While East Coast locomotive men always claimed that the three all-roller-bearing Peppercorn class A1 Pacifics were superior to the rest of the class, no one in motive power depots or workshops seems to have established any marked distinction between the three groups of Britannia Pacifics in this context.

The two Britannias which the Southern retained until the summer of 1958, nos. 70004/14, were always Eastern Section residents of Stewarts Lane, but the BR Pacifics did have a stab at some of the Western Section's principal duties in April and May 1953. The reason was a stop order on all Bulleid Merchant Navy Pacifics pending ultrasonic axle examination after no. 35020 had fractured a driving axle and derailed near Crewkerne with the 2.20 pm Ilfracombe–Waterloo on 24 April. Amongst the temporary substitutes loaned to the SR, which included some Gresley V2 2–6–2s, were five of the WR Britannias, of which nos. 70017/23 were assigned to Salisbury and nos. 70024/8/9 to Exmouth Junction. Nos. 70030/4 from the LMR's Longsight depot were sent to Stewarts Lane to cover for missing Eastern Section Merchant Navies.

The move of nos. 70004/14 from Stewarts Lane was part of the first comprehensive inter-Regional transfer of the Pacifics since their debut. Throughout 1958 the LMR had been bending BR headquarters' ears to its need of more class 7 power on its Western Division. What it wanted was to gather there more of the Royal Scot 4–6–0s, especially those operating the length of the Midland main line from St Pancras to Carlisle. To replace the Scots on the Midland, so the gossip ran, the LM management had suggested that the East Coast Regions might be induced to part with some V2 2–6–2s (this got as far as clearance-testing a Neasden V2 between Cricklewood and the East Midlands that summer) or A2 4–6–2s. The LMR was even prepared to try its hand with some Bulleid light Pacifics from the SR's generous stock. In the event the Midland got Britannias – the SR pair, nos. 70015–21 from the WR and 70042 from the ER, all of which were initially allocated to Manchester's Trafford Park depot. This move was soon followed by a switch to Leeds Holbeck shed – by now an NER depot – of Scotland's nos. 70053–4, which were joined soon afterwards by no. 70044 from the LMR. The Holbeck engines, naturally, were essentially intended for Midland main line duty, but on 10 December 1958 no. 70053 was sent experimentally to the Yorkshire coast on the 8.42 am Bradford Forster Square–Scarborough.

Enginemen on the LMR's Western Division seldom realised the full potential of their Britannias because few thought to adjust their driving method to the prodigious steam-making capacity of the Pacifics' boilers. As a result they tended to rate the Pacifics as inferior to the Royal Scot 4–6–0s, which were usually the Britannias' work roster partners. Top link Midland men were much more adaptable. Consequently their acquisition of Britannias for the St Pancras–Manchester trains, by now operated without intermediate engine change at Derby, added fresh lustre to the image of the class which GE engine crews had created at the start of the 1950s.

Most likely some Midland man qualified the design for membership of the 100 mph club, but the highest speed on the tempting Bedford dip authenticated by one of the railway journals' accepted recorders fell just short of a 'ton' at 99 mph. That was by no. 70032 at the head of a nine-coach, 320 ton northbound train chasing 5 minutes squandered in signal and permanent way checks in the London suburbs, which reached this peak at the foot of the 5½ miles of 1 in 202 down to Flitwick in the process of averaging close on 90 mph for 17.2 miles from Leagrave to Bedford. In the reverse direction another sparkling performance of the many that were published featuring speeds in the higher 90s between Sharnbrook summit and Leagrave, had no. 70014 making a net time of 87½ minutes, as against a 99 minute schedule, over the 99.1 miles from Leicester to St Pancras with a peak of 95 mph on the downhill sprint from Sharnbrook.

Throughout its period on the Midland no. 70014 was a highly respected engine, though its debut had been unpropitious. On its third St Pancras–Manchester trip with the 'Palatine' it had parted company with tender and train between Hazel Grove and Cheadle Heath – not

G W Morrison

10. Sad spectacle: shorn of nameplates, filthy and far from steamtight, no. 70000, 'Britannia', near the end of her career, finds work on the trans-Pennine route, heading a Saturday Leeds–Llandudno train out of Huddersfield past Gledholt Junction on 10 March 1965.

the first such occurrence with the class, but one which was supposed to have been forestalled by the addition of safety links after half-a-dozen or more such failures with the GE engines. But for the one-piece footplate they could have been fatal for Britannia firemen, while the driver's anxiety was how to stop his engine. Severance of the brake-pipe automatically clapped brakes on disappearing tender and train, but there was no way of isolating a Britannia's steam brake, so that putting the engine into reverse was about the only course open.

Another alarming Midland line incident happened on a January night in 1960 when no. 70052, heading the 9.05 pm Glasgow St Enoch–St Pancras over the Pennines, shed both right-hand bottom slidebars. Whereafter the severely stressed piston rod shattered on the descent from Blea Moor, releasing the connecting rod to saw the air and lash the ballast. Incredibly the Pacific itself was not levered off the track, but the flailing rod did such damage to the neighbouring track-bed that an oncoming northbound freight on the down line was derailed. This, too, was not a first occurrence, but until then the application of modified fastenings to obviate it had been lethargic. Only four Pacifics had been treated and no. 70052 was not one of them. Now the whole class (and the Clan Pacifics) were quickly taken in hand.

Midland main line duty was the last high point in the Britannias' career. Total dieselisation of the GE line at the start of the 1960s set off the first of a sequence of retreats to regroup on new ground in face of oncoming battalions of new traction.

In the GE line's 1958 summer timetable all but four of the London–Norwich expresses were rostered for diesel traction, which freed Britannias to implement a smartly accelerated Clacton–Liverpool Street service as a curtain-raiser to this route's electrification. Ipswich and Yarmouth South Town crews had regular use of the Pacifics for some East Suffolk line trains, and March men their first example for a regular working to York and back with the through Colchester–Newcastle service. These final months of Britannia operation in East Anglia also produced the longest daily duty rostered for a GE line Pacific, a 505-mile turn which every 24 hours took an engine from London's Goodmayes yard to Harwich Parkeston Quay on continental freight, from Harwich to Sheffield Victoria and back on the boat train, once titled the 'North Country Continental', then back to London on an up night freight from Parkeston Quay. By the summer of 1961 seven of the original GE line Britannias had each amassed more than 700,000 miles in a decade.

At the end of 1961 distribution of the Britannias had undergone almost complete metamorphosis. The core of the GE line was down to just three Pacifics, all at Norwich (which assumed maintenance responsibility for all GE Britannias when Stratford started to dieselise in the late 1950s), and most of the original GE batch had moved on to March, which had eleven and would soon relieve Norwich of its final trio. At the start of the year three of the later batch of GE Britannias had been moved to Immingham to supplant B1 4–6–0s on the Cleethorpes–King's Cross expresses, and by the year's end that depot had seven, nos. 70035–41.

Diesels had ousted the Cardiff Canton Pacifics, and seven of them, along with nos. 70031 and 70043, had been extradited to the LMR's West Midlands shed of Aston to serve as freight power (by then the frequent lot of the LMR's Stanier Pacifics too). Six others had been sent to Carlisle sheds. Holyhead had been deprived of its five Britannias at the close of 1959 and for some months most of them were at Newton Heath, relieving Jubilee 4–6–0s on the Manchester–Glasgow trains, but also covering short-haul passenger turns between Manchester and Colne, Accrington, Southport and Todmorden. Their quota of this less demanding work increased as their condition deteriorated, until late in 1961 the trio, nos. 70045/8/9, was ordered south to inaugurate Britannia haulage of the miserable Marylebone–Nottingham rump of Great Central passenger service from Neasden depot. Ironically, all three returned to Holyhead early in 1963, when five Pacifics were posted to that shed, and a further five to Llandudno Junction in one of the final moves to find work for the type. Others of the class had a share of the GC passenger trains almost to the latter's death in the mid-1960s.

At the end of 1960 the LMR tired of the loosened bolts and rivets, and the strained smokebox saddle fitments and main frame cross-stretchers, sustained by the Midland's Britannias in pounding up the grades of the Derby–Manchester main line. All were exchanged for Western lines' Royal Scots, though one or two Britannias did tread the Midland again in the later 1960s when that route was bearing the brunt of the Manchester–London passenger service during the painful electrification of the main line from Euston to the north-west.

11. Back on the main line where the Polmadie-based Britannias in their prime regularly worked the Glasgow–Manchester/Liverpool trains, the now un-named nos. 70013 and 70039 double-head a summer Saturday Euston–Glasgow extra near Shap on 31 July 1965.

Derek Cross

The rest of the Britannia story is one of steady degradation, both of condition and work. First to be scrapped were nos. 70007/44 in 1965, the year when one final new home for the type was found at Oxley shed. Where the engines were useful as supplementary power for summer extras to the West Country, but were otherwise used mostly on freight and parcels haulage. In the 1966–7 winter several Britannias were thought worth a further overhaul and repaint at Crewe works – no. 70013 was in fact the last steam locomotive to get the treatment there – but at the end of 1967 the last thirteen were taken out of operational service.

Withdrawn in 1966, the prototype no. 70000

'Britannia' was laid aside for preservation by the BR Board, but it was severely vandalised while in store and no. 70013 was selected instead. It was kept in working order throughout the first half of 1968 and was turned out for the Manchester–Carlisle leg of the notoriously high-priced 'Last Steam' special run by BR on 11 August that year. Thereafter it was passed to the Bressingham Steam Museum for permanent preservation.

Optimism ran high that a Britannia would once more be hauling passengers in the autumn of 1978. The spurned 'Britannia' herself had been purchased by the Britannia Locomotive Society, and in the spring of 1971 transported to the privately run Severn Valley Railway at Bridgnorth for rehabilitation as a working locomotive. At last, in May 1978, she was ready for steaming and her parent, Robin Riddles, was invited to rename her before an enthusiastic gathering at Bridgnorth.

But the chance to ride once more behind 'Britannia' on BR had to be a pleasure deferred. A welded repair to the inside of the outer firebox failed to pass the BR boiler inspector's scrutiny. Before BR would let the engine on to their tracks no. 70000's owners faced a very costly dismantling of the firebox to remake the repair.

In the spring of 1980 the Britannia Locomotive Society transferred no. 70000 to the Nene Valley Railway at Peterborough for further efforts to restore the Pacific to acceptable condition for current main line steam operation (and also for equipment with air braking). Sadly it was not ready for such employment in 1981 and – at the time of writing – although able to work trains on the Nene Valley Railway, was not figuring in the list of additional locomotives to power main line steam excursions in 1982.

Examples preserved:
Class 7 4–6–2 nos.
70000 Nene Valley Railway
70013 Bressingham Steam Museum

3
The Class 6 Pacifics

The case for a standard class 6 4–6–2 was never compelling. An outline standard locomotive programme of June 1948 had suggested a step up to the 4–6–2 layout for a type to succeed all the pre-nationalisation class 5 4–6–0 designs – LNER class B1, LMS Black Five, and GWR County and Hall. However, mature consideration questioned whether the percentage of these engines' normal work which overstretched their capacity was high enough to warrant a general resort to ten or eleven more tons of locomotive weight in the new design. True, a Pacific's bigger firebox would result in more economical working on the common run of class 5 work which would not extend a 4–6–2; but calculations showed that these savings would be neatly cancelled out by the recurring depreciation and maintenance costs of the bigger engines. All in all, debits outweighed gains and the 4–6–0 arrangement was perpetuated for class 5 construction.

On the other hand, though their mechanical intricacies and extravagant habits were anathema to the Railway Executive team's creed of mechanical simplicity and thermal economy, Bulleid's 'West Country' Pacifics had undoubtedly made a case for the more powerful design on at least one weight-restricted route during the 1948 Exchanges. Now legendary are the performances of no. 34004, 'Yeovil', over the Highland line between Perth and Inverness, especially its epic climb of 'The Hill' from Blair Atholl to Struan, of which almost 3 miles slope at about 1 in 80. The Southern engine strode so impetuously up to 46 mph on this incline that it winded the ex-Caledonian 4–4–0 banking at the rear of the 380-ton train. The load that day was well in excess of the 255-ton limit for a single Stanier class 5 4–6–0, which necessitated double-heading of the 'Royal Highlander' sleeper at least every day of the year and of a considerable proportion of the Highland's passenger services in the summer season. So with this and other Scottish routes in mind, plus possibly the Great Central main line and ex-LMS Jubilee duties on the LMR, the Railway Executive team decided there was a place in the standard fleet for a class 6 rather than a class 5 Pacific.

Preoccupation with the standardisation of as many mechanical components as possible between types in the new fleet seems to have deterred the Railway Executive men from detailed consideration of other wheel arrangements. For the severe switchbacks of the Scottish Highlands above all, many critics at the time would have opted for an eight-coupled design. But it was only in later years that Riddles himself conceded that a 4–8–0 with around 72 tons of adhesion weight would have

12. Class 6 4–6–2 no. 72000, 'Clan Buchanan', as built. *Cecil J Allen Collection*

been a more productive addition to the standard range than the class 6 4–6–2.

Instead, the class 6 was built up from the class 7 4–6–2 chassis, with identical driving wheel diameter and wheel spacing. To this was fitted a smaller boiler (type BR2) than that of the class 7, with 36 as against 42 sq. ft of grate area, 225 rather than 250 lb/sq. in. boiler pressure and a 35 instead of a 40-element superheater. That saved 5½ tons of engine weight compared with the Britannia and kept the class 6 within the 19-ton axle-load limit, but with the inevitable penalty of inferior adhesion weight. Another difference from the class 7 was that in the smaller 4–6–2 cylinder diameter was contracted to 19½ in. The tender was the BR1 model as paired with the first batch of class 7 4–6–2s.

The parent office for the class 6 4–6–2 was Derby and what was envisaged as only the first series, nos. 72000–9, emerged between December 1951 and April 1952. All were named after Scottish Clans, reinforcing the belief that their assignment would be north of the Forth–Clyde valley. But the first five were allocated to Glasgow Polmadie, the remainder to Carlisle Kingmoor, and there they stayed for most of their career.

One of the Kingmoor stud, no. 72007, introduced the type to Inverness in August 1952, but thereafter Clan forays on the Highland line were very sporadic and presumably the unpremeditated results of extempore rostering. Four years later a Clan also set wheel on the West Highland line. In mid-June that year the Cameron clan rallied at Achnasherry Castle, near Spean Bridge, the seat of its chieftain, The Cameron of Lochiel, who also happened to serve part-time

13. The class 6 4–6–2s are remembered chiefly for their duty on the Glasgow–NW England expresses: no. 72004, 'Clan Macdonald', heads the midday service from Manchester to Edinburgh and Glasgow over Tebay troughs on 5 August 1955.

Cecil J Allen Collection

on the British Transport Commission. That no doubt bent accommodating minds to a suggestion that the clansmen be borne from Glasgow Queen Street to Spean Bridge behind their eponymous class 6 Pacific, no. 72001 (and to a still more particular request: the eventual Special Notice for the day stipulated that none but simon-pure Camerons man the engine). So, after a clearance test early in May, no. 72001 was drafted to West Highland work for a whole June week, of which the Cameron special was the centrepiece, and Fort William was granted its first glimpse of a Pacific. West Highland enginemen, it was reported, discounted this as a privilege, grumbling that no. 72001 rode roughly and ground hard into the route's sharp curves.

Throughout the 1950s the Polmadie engines' main employment was on the Glasgow–Manchester/Liverpool expresses, plus duty over the routes from Glasgow to Perth, Dundee, and as far as Aberdeen. The Kingmoor Clans' assignments included a number in ex-Glasgow & South Western territory, of which the toughest was a diagram covering the heavy Stranraer sleeper each way beyond Carlisle, with an intermediate Glasgow leg on the 11.44 am from Stranraer and the 5.10 pm back from St Enoch. Occasionally the Clans also travelled the Clyde coast lines.

Categorised as mixed traffic engines, the Clans never really warranted that billing. With no more adhesion weight than a Black Five 4–6–0 (and less than that of a Jubilee 4–6–0) they did not have the sureness of foot for heavier freight haulage. Correctly handled, they steamed comfortably enough and with satisfactory economy of coal and water consumption on moderately loaded trains – in fact, some Carlisle and Glasgow crews found them easier machines to live with than the Britannias, especially after the Clans' steaming had been improved by a marginal narrowing of their blastpipes in 1953–4 to create a draught strength nearer the boiler's potential output. But whereas Kingmoor enginemen had few complaints at their Clans' way with the more modestly loaded Glasgow–Stranraer trains, the fierce switchback of that route south of Girvan notwithstanding, they would happily have reverted to Jubilee 4–6–0s for the long climb to Gatehouse of Fleet with the heavier Euston–Stranraer boat trains. The only reason ever made public for the Scottish Region's disinclination to deploy the Clans permanently in the Highlands is that the latter's class 5 4–6–0s were all of recent build, and that therefore the cost of transferring their single-line tablet exchange apparatus to the Pacifics was not warranted. That the sum involved would have been a deterrent had the 4–6–2s been markedly superior to the 4–6–0s for Highland work stretches credulity.

A further fifteen class 6 Pacifics were to have been built in 1954, ten of them for Scotland and, extraordinarily in view of its surfeit of Bulleid light Pacifics, five for the SR. A list of clan names for the Scottish engines and of five resurrected titles of historic SR steam power forerunners – 'Hengist', 'Horsa', 'Canute', 'Wildfire' and 'Firebrand' – was in fact publicised by the BR administration before nos. 72010–24 suddenly faded from the BR forward building programme without explanation. The reason did not become plain until the following year's fanfares for BR's 1955 Modernisation Plan and its switch to diesel locomotion. Although steam building was to continue, there was obviously no justification for prolonging the production line of a purely express passenger locomotive such as the class 6 had proved to be.

In the later 1950s the London Midland was still reaping the bitter harvest of its forerunners' reluctance to follow the neighbours' line in the 1930s and 1940s and accumulate an ample stud of class 7 and 8 power. Steady acceleration and intensification of the express service from St Pancras to the East Midlands and Yorkshire had the Region's operators desperate to avoid plundering the West Coast main line's stud of Royal Scot 4–6–0s, and anxiously canvassing the chances of extracting Peppercorn or Britannia Pacifics from the East Coast, even Bulleid Pacifics from the Southern. Class 6 Clan Pacifics from time to time deputed to Leeds workings from Carlisle and then appropriated for a Midland main line duty had not kindled any belief that they would be a present help in trouble.

The argument for an Eastern Region surrender of Britannias looked unassailable when, in the reconstruction of its 1958 summer timetable to embody dieselisation of the London–Ipswich–Norwich service with its first deliveries of class 31 and 40 units, the ER planned to redeploy the ousted Britannias on the short-haul Liverpool Street–Clacton route. BR headquarters agreed there was a case to answer, and in September 1958 the ER was bidden to give one of the LMR's Kingmoor-based Clans, no.

Derek Cross

14. Another regular Clan Pacific sphere of duty: no. 72007, 'Clan Mackintosh', takes water during the Ayr stop of the Stranraer–Newcastle boat train on 7 August 1965.

72009, a month's stint from Stratford depot on the Clacton trains.

However, Liverpool Street had also reshaped this service; and partly for commercial reasons, partly for a good operating marriage with the dieselised Norwich workings, it had been accelerated close to the margin of class 7 steam traction. Soon finding the Clan no better than a B1 4–6–0 in reasonable condition, the Stratford enginemen had to hammer the class 6 to keep touch with schedule. In mid-October no. 72009 limped back to the LMR and the projected transfer of all five LMR Clans to Stratford in exchange for Britannias never materialised.

In 1958 four Clans, nos. 72000/2/5/6, were given a spell at Edinburgh's Haymarket depot, principally for work over the Waverley route to Carlisle (subsequently one of the controversial main line closures of the Beeching era). The class 6 Pacifics also took a share of the turns from Edinburgh Waverley to Glasgow Queen Street, including the 'Queen of Scots' Pullman, and were assigned to some Dundee–Aberdeen rosters, including the diagram covering the down 'Night Scotsman'. Haymarket crews did not relish the Clans as an alternative to East

Coast Pacifics and V2 2–6–2s, voicing sharp criticism both of the BR engines' comparatively sluggish performance and of their limited tender water capacity against that of an LNER eight-wheeler. Nevertheless, for one or two subsequent years Polmadie customarily loaned most of its quintet to Haymarket and St Margarets sheds for a couple of spring months to create spare traction capacity for the annual seed potato traffic.

These Edinburgh tours apart, the Clans stayed put at Polmadie and Kingmoor. For the rest of their career they attracted attention only for the abnormal jobs for which sheds sometimes purloined them between out and home legs of their base depot diagrams. Newton Heath depot found the Polmadie engines useful for a wide range of short-haul passenger trips between Manchester Victoria and the rest of Lancashire, including Blackpool. Needless to say the first day or two following a Crewe works visit for attention could find a Clan loosening up on trains heading anywhere from Euston to the Cumbrian coast.

Clans were most frequently seen in the south after the spring 1959 upgrading of the 8.35 pm Stirling–Sutton Coldfield Motorail to a class 6 duty. That regularly put a Kingmoor Clan in the hands of Birmingham's Aston shed and was the cause of no. 72005 making the type's WR debut at Bristol on 8 July 1960 with the Friday 8.45 pm Bradford–Paignton, which the Clan had taken over at Birmingham; it returned north next day on the 7.45 am Paignton–Newcastle. Much later, in the twilight of BR steam on 15 April 1964, no. 72006 even got beyond the Severn Tunnel to Margam yard with an overnight oil empties from Carlisle.

By then all Polmadie's Clans had been scrapped in a Scottish Region holocaust of 213 steam locomotives during the last four weeks of 1962 (this also eliminated the Royal Scot and Jubilee 4–6–0s from Scottish sheds and condemned the first three Stanier Duchess Pacifics). Surprisingly the Kingmoor engines survived almost to the death of Scottish steam in general. The last trio was not withdrawn until 1966.

4
The Class 8 Pacific

But for the appalling triple collision at Harrow & Wealdstone in October 1952 the BR standard class 8 4–6–2 would almost certainly not have got beyond the drawing board. Until then the type had not figured in any published production programme. It had sensibly been given a low priority in the construction plan, for considering the impoverished levels of speed permitted by the state of the track and other equipment in the early post-war years, the stock of inherited, custom-built class 8P power was adequate for the immediate future.

As the 1950s progressed most realists recognised that Canute-like British resistance to the tide of dieselisation and electrification elsewhere in the industrial world was becoming untenable. The BR class 8P looked more and more like a chimerical proposition. But the destruction at Harrow of no. 46202, 'Princess Anne', the orthodox rebuild of the former LMS Turbomotive Pacific, presented Riddles with a pretext for adding a new class 8P to stock. Although the BTC must surely have known that the chances of BR ever needing a new breed of express passenger Pacific had become slim, it accepted Riddles' plea that a prototype was worth building to get all the design parameters right through practical running experience before any demand for mass production arose.

E. S. Cox's draft programme had sketched the class 8 roughly as a revamped Stanier Duchess Pacific, but with bar frames and a WD-style eight-wheel tender to hold 10 tons of coal and 5,000 gallons of water, which would have given it a wider operational range than the LMS 4–6–2s. Their representatives in the 1948 Locomotive Exchanges had been forced to unhook their 4,000 gallon six-wheel tenders in favour of a WD eight-wheeler before attacking the SR's Waterloo–Salisbury–Exeter route, with its lack of water troughs.

Other ideas surfaced when the nod came for a class 8 prototype to be built. Invited in 1953 to block out a firm design, Derby conceived a hybrid in which the influential hands of the LMR's new mechanical chief from Doncaster, J. F. ('Freddy') Harrison, and the Derby drawing office chief from Eastleigh, C. S. Cock, were patent. With a smoke-deflectored, Merchant Navy-type boiler feeding three cylinders mounted on a Britannia-style chassis with 6 ft 2 in. driving wheels, it looked rather like a Bulleid reshaping of the LNER Peppercorn A2 Pacific subsequently unfrocked by BR.

Riddles' team in London preferred to remould the Britannia design, partly for the advantage of some commonality in mechanical parts. Hence the class 8 took shape with a Britannia boiler, though with slightly reduced

15. The unique class 8 4–6–2 no. 71000, 'Duke of Gloucester'.

Cecil J Allen Collection

superheating surface, a double blastpipe and chimney, and a bigger firebox, with 48.6 sq. ft of grate area and 226 sq. ft of heating surface, as against the class 7's 42 and 210 sq. ft respectively. The class 8 firebox was a foot longer than the class 7's and extended into the boiler barrel to form a combustion chamber. The Britannia's 6 ft 2 in. driving wheel dimension was retained, since any hidebound theory that 6 ft 6 in. at least was de rigueur in a type consistently assigned to fast passenger work had been demolished by Bulleid's Southern and Peppercorn's East Coast class A2 Pacifics, if not by the Britannias themselves. All driving axles were given roller bearings.

Two cylinders ample enough to generate the power in mind would have infringed clearances, so the class 8 was given three (an arrangement preferred to four on grounds of more even turning moment). The rejected Derby draft had resorted to a Merchant Navy-type boiler partly because the latter's bottom-side, as opposed to the customary top-side taper, simplified the contrivance of an orthodox valve gear and middle axle drive for the inside cylinder. The finally authorised version solved the space problem by resorting to the compactness of Caprotti poppet valve gear, which had impressed Riddles when he was closely involved in the LMS rebuilding of a number ex-LNWR Claughton 4–6–0s with it. Its intrinsic merits as a valve gear apart, the Caprotti system was quite critical to the economics of the class 8 prototype; without it Riddles would almost certainly have faced the expense of designing and building a special, one-off boiler for the multi-cylinder Pacific.

The class 8 tender was certainly a one-off, adapted from one taken from the class 9 2–10–0 production line. Designated BR1J, it had 10 tons coal and 4,325 gallons water capacity. It was also equipped for the fireman's benefit with a steam powered coal-pusher, of the type Stanier had devised for his LMS Duchess Pacifics. That helped to lift the tender weight in working order to 55½ tons, over 6 tons more than the gross of the first Britannias' type BR1.

Named 'Duke of Gloucester', class 8 no. 71000 eventually materialised from Crewe works in the spring of 1954. That was just in time for it to feature in a large display of up-to-date BR traction, from specimen standard steam types to a WR gas turbine, an SR main line diesel and a Manchester–Sheffield dc electric, which was staged in the Willesden shed roundhouse for delegates to that year's London session of the International Railway Congress.

Throughout the summer no. 71000 was given a carefully controlled induction by Crewe North depot, to which the engine was attached throughout its life. In late June and early July it was assigned to some customary Crewe running-in turns of the day, such as the 8.10 am Windermere–Manchester and the 3.53 pm Manchester–Barrow, and a working to Blackpool, returning to Crewe on the 2.50 pm fish train from Wyre Dock. Not until early October was the 'Duke' passed for routine assignment to the depot's class 8 Pacific rosters in which the 'Mid-day Scot' and 'West Coast Postal' were prominent. Apart from overnight sleepers these were the only front-rank trains between Euston and Scotland to change engines at Crewe instead of Carlisle. South of Crewe the Pacific heading the up early morning 'Postal' returned with the 'Mid-day Scot', while the down 'Postal' was covered by the Pacific taking on the same morning's up Inverness sleeper, due out of Crewe at 5.02 am.

When the 'Duke' was commissioned the down 'Mid-day Scot' was about the toughest weekday locomotive assignment in the country, booked over the 82.6 miles to its first stop at Rugby in 80 minutes despite a loading of fourteen and sometimes fifteen coaches aggregating just under or over 510 tons, passengers included. Some drivers managed the transition from a Stanier Pacific and kept time quite comfortably with the 'Duke', demonstrating that once under way it could be urged up to 90 mph on the slopes north of Tring. Others lost time badly, unable to adapt their driving habits to the different characteristics of the Riddles machine. Complaints of the 'Duke's' inordinate appetite for coal, though, were almost unanimous: so was preference for a Stanier Pacific.

In 1955 no. 71000 was submitted to the BTC's locomotive efficiency test routines, in this case under the tutelage of the Swindon team, which examined the Pacific both on their stationary plant and in controlled load trials on the open track. This examination awarded maximum points to everything that turned the Pacific's steam into tractive power. Cylinder efficiency, in fact, was claimed to surpass that of any other simple expansion locomotive for which test records were available, anywhere in the world. The shortcomings which made the locomotive's performance such a lottery were in the boiler.

Fed by two firemen with coal at the rate of 7,000 lb an hour the 'Duke' could only generate 34,000 lb of steam an hour, whereas a Britannia had managed 37,560 lb and a Bulleid Merchant Navy 42,000 lb. Once the firing rate was stepped above about 4,000 lb an hour, the 'Duke' started to spew unburnt coal out of the chimney like a shower of glowing oranges. In

16. The 'Duke' undergoing tests on the stationary plant at Swindon works. *Cecil J Allen Collection*

general, the conclusion was that whenever an exceptional power output was asked of it, the 'Duke' would probably consume 12 per cent more coal than the rest of the British 4–6–2 classes. Once the steam was generated, however, the efficiency of the machinery below the boiler was patent; throughout the trials no. 71000's cut-off was never higher than 20 per cent – the examiners found, in fact, that the Pacific could be worked with cut-off dropped as low as 5 per cent.

The complementary road trials of the day's steam locomotive testing procedures aimed to reproduce as nearly as possible the constants simulated on the stationary plant, and to set the locomotive at them with its output at a stable level, controlled as closely as it had been on the rollers, to see how far practice corroborated what had been learned in artificial conditions.

Brunel's main line outside the Swindon works doorstep, with its near-immaculate grading and alignment, was ideal for such strictly controlled exercises, which were conducted with loads stepped up gradually to twenty coaches, sometimes even more. Correlation of the data from the two phases of testing produced indices of performance for a number of major classes that were the most reliable guides to efficient timetabling British passenger service planners had ever had in the steam age.

The 'Duke' was duly road-tested between Swindon and Westbury via the Reading West Curve. With 459 tons in tow it burned coal at a rate of 3,139 lb an hour to sustain 75–76 mph on the level, but when the trailing load was augmented to 586 tons the Pacific had to be fired at almost 2¼ tons an hour to hold 78–80 mph on the flat. On these tests the drawbar horsepowers recorded were inferior to those noted with Britannia no. 70005 for equivalent rates of coal consumption and steam production.

The private chagrin of Riddles and his aides must have been considerable when the cold print of the test data proved that they had somehow failed to produce a boiler that generated the heat expected from its coal-burning capacity, considering that the achievement of fast-steaming boilers was among the major credits of some of their European predecessors. Some experts, lay as well as professional, suspected that the cause was connected with the use of poppet valves, the rapid exhaust opening of which imparted a much sharper draught on the exhaust gases than piston valves. There was evidence that this had a marked effect on the steaming of simple expansion engines, notably in the findings of the tests of the poppet-valve Gresley 2–8–2 'Cock o' the North' on French Railways' Vitry plant before the war, but Riddles and his men do not appear to have consulted these records.

So the root causes of the 'Duke's' failure to realise its full potential, even when attentively handled, had not been discovered when, in 1956, mass production of the design was canvassed at BR headquarters. With the benefit of hindsight it seems incredible that the idea should have been seriously advanced when the prototype Deltic was already operational and opening up a new horizon of feasible inter-city speed; but the fallibility and the limited capability of the 'pilot scheme' main line diesels were bending receptive ears to the committed steam engineers' argument that this form of traction needed a longer period of development and BR more experience with it before serious contracts were placed. At the end of the day, of course, the steam faction lost the vote. If they had not, there would surely have been no production Deltics.

For the rest of its short life no. 71000 rarely figured in either the text or the illustration of the railway press. By 1962, when Stanier's Princess Royal Pacifics were going to the scrapheap and some of his Duchesses into store, the odds were heavily weighted against the BR class 8's survival, if only because of the mounting cost of keeping a singleton in repair. The 'Duke' was in fact still serviceable when it was withdrawn in November 1962. The BTC had the previous year scheduled it for preservation intact, but this decision was now annulled in favour of retaining only the inside Caprotti valve gear and cylinder layout as a museum-piece. The rest of the engine joined the melancholy hulks sold to Woodham Bros of Barry as scrap metal.

Almost eleven years later the rusting shell of the 'Duke', shorn of most of its external fittings, was bought from Woodhams for £4,950 by a group of enthusiasts and transported to Main Line Steam Trust's base on the former Great Central line at Loughborough for restoration to working order. Even if no. 71000 had been one of a numerous class these dedicated people

17. The 'Duke' at work: no. 71000 clambers up Camden bank with the 7.10 pm 'Northern Irishman' boat train from Euston in May 1962.

M Pope

would have set themselves a daunting job, considering the forlorn, skeletal state to which it had deteriorated. But since it had so many unique features they were arguably addressing the most taxing restoration yet attempted.

So thoroughly have they researched the job that it seems they may have identified the flaws in the design which either eluded BR in the Pacific's working life or were else not thought worth probing. Writing in *Railway World* Peter King, a Councillor of the 71000 ('Duke of Gloucester') Steam Locomotive Trust Ltd, has described how the likely reasons came to light for the engine's known idiosyncrasy: that when effort was asked of it the firebed seriously deteriorated and fragmented, letting unburnt coal be sucked into the boiler tubes and ejected with the exhaust.

Restoration of the engine to steaming state demanded a new ashpan. Lacking no. 71000's original drawings at the start of their work, the new owners had to work from the decayed ashpan they found in the engine, but by the time the replacement was manufactured they had come into possession of the authentic BR drawings. Checking their replacement against these the restorers were astonished to discover that the damper door spaces in the original fitment had been botched in manufacture. Compared with specification there was a discrepancy of no less than 6 sq. ft. No wonder the draught of air through the grate had been inadequate – something that BR's engineers had suspected but dismissed as impossible in view of the provision they had made for it.

Next the restorers unearthed an historical nonsense which will have drawn a derisive snort from any Eastern Region steam power man who read Peter King's piece, as similar obstinancy nearly ruined the double-chimney transformation of the Gresley A3 and A4 Pacifics. The manufacturers of the British Caprotti valve gear had urged that the 'Duke' be fitted with a Kylchap double blastpipe and chimney as the most appropriate device to temper the sharp exhaust effect of their poppet valves. But the BR men insisted on fitting the Swindon design of plain double blastpipe and chimney – as they tried to impose on the Gresley A4s, happily in vain – despite the vigorous objections of the Caprotti experts that this would aggravate the harshness of the poppet valve exhaust. The 'Duke's' new owners seem pretty certain that the Caprotti view was right. The combined effect of the unsuitable blastpipe and the wrongly-manufactured ashpan could well have been to disintegrate the firebed and inhibit efficient combustion.

Sadly one doubts that BR will give the eventually restored and revised 'Duke' the scope to prove that, with every detail right, it was the potential 'world-beater' in steam traction efficiency anticipated by its designers.

5
The Mixed Traffic 4–6–0s

Once it had been decided to develop the mixed traffic class 5 as a 4–6–0 rather than a 4–6–2, for reasons outlined in the preceding chapter, the standard design's main source of inspiration was easily predictable. Never mind the LMS provenance of the Riddles team's senior members, the LMS Black Five as designed by Stanier and refined by Ivatt was unarguably one of the supremely successful answers to an operating specification in British traction history, coupling a wide route availability with efficient steaming and the mechanical competence for 90 mph on express passenger work.

For the standard class 5 4–6–0, therefore, the Stanier class 5 boiler was adopted almost intact, retaining the LMS type's 225 lb/sq. in. pressure. That was married to the same pattern of cylinders, valve gear and driving wheels as used in the class 6 4–6–2, save that in the class 5 the cylinder diameter was reduced from the Pacific's 19½ in. to 19 in. The 6 ft 2 in. driving wheels were 2 in. bigger than those of the Stanier Black Five, which in prospect gladdened LMR engineers who felt that a little more length of leg would have added a crowning touch to the LMS design, given its clear superiority to some purpose-built express engines on many medium-load inter-city turns. Total engine weight was 76.2 tons and maximum axle load 19.7 tons.

The parent office for the class 5 design was Doncaster, which also built twenty-five of the engines in 1955–6 and the final seventeen of the type in 1956–7. The rest were all erected at Derby. As with the class 7 Pacifics, tender design was varied to suit Regional assignments.

The first forty-nine, of which thirty-nine went to the LMR and the remainder to Scotland, were, like the first class 7 4–6–2s, paired with the BR1 tender, but then came the first variation with the SR's initial trio, nos. 73050–2, which were sent to Bath to introduce the type to the Somerset & Dorset line in mid-1954; they were given the 5,000 gallon BR1G tender created that year for the first ten 2–10–0s. With no. 73065, the first of a second flock of class 5s for the LM and Scottish Regions, the initial pattern of tender with inset bunker for improved rearward look-out gave way to flush-sided designs, in this case the BR1C with coal capacity raised from 7 to 9 tons. Here one might interpolate that the first batches of the 4–6–0s were turned out with BR chime whistles as fitted to the Britannias, which were at first mounted behind the chimney. Before long, however, new class 5s were emerging with the whistle in more familiar position on the firebox top. In final deliveries

18. The class 5 4–6–0 as built: in immaculate lined black livery no. 73005 heads the Aberdeen-bound 'Granite City' out of Glasgow Buchanan Street past St Rollox on 16 June 1952.

Cecil J Allen Collection

the chimes were replaced by standard whistles.

The second batch of SR class 5s, nos. 73080–90, and some further Scottish examples, nos. 73100–9 and 73120–34, were turned out with the flush-sided, 7 tons coal-capacity BR1B. The final change was the choice of the otherwise exclusively 2–10–0 tender, the BR1F with maximum 5,625 gallons of water capacity but only 7 tons' coal space, for nos. 73110–9, to suit them for the SR's Western Section main line, which was devoid of water troughs.

The prototype, no. 73000, was displayed to Railway Executive brass and the press at Marylebone on 26 April 1951 as a prelude to the allocation of the first five LMR engines to East Midlands sheds and the first Scottish quintet to Perth South. The assignment of a couple to Derby shed quickly introduced the type to centres as far apart as Bristol and York – in fact, one penetrated to Scarborough as early as June that year on a Saturday excursion. And as early as 3 August a Perth pair, nos. 73005/6, graduated to Royal duty, double-heading the Royal train from their home station to Aberdeen. As for normal duty the Perth class 5s were immediately covering both the Highland line to Inverness and principal passenger turns to both Glasgow and Aberdeen. Chester, Patricroft and Blackpool sheds were the recipients of the final engines from the initial batch of thirty, Blackpool giving Euston its first sight of standard class 5s by trying them on what had previously been Jubilee jobs.

T G Hepburn/Rail Archive Stephenson

19. Two of the Midland line-based class 5 4–6–0s were initially fitted with a Westinghouse pump for the Toton–Brent brake-fitted coal train trials: one of them, no. 73030, leaves Nottingham with a St Pancras express in the 1950s.

Many areas got an unexpectedly early acquaintance with the new class 5s as a result of their appropriation to cover emergencies. When the Britannia Pacifics were immobilised for rectification of the early failings that ended up in loosened driving wheels nos. 73000/2 were sent from the Midland line early in November 1951 to help out at the ER's Stratford shed. Despite the substitutes' lower power classification, the Great Eastern men were clearly more at home on the class 5s than on their other stop-gaps, a trio of Bulleid light Pacifics from the SR. The latter were rarely turned out for the principal Britannia diagrams, whereas the class 5s were consistently marked up for them. While they could not match Britannia effort their work was generally well up to the best pre-war performance of the Gresley three-cylinder B17 4–6–0s.

In May 1953 three other Midland-based class 5s, nos. 73003/15/8, were sequestered, along with seven Stanier Black Fives from the LMR,

G F Heiron

20. One of the later series of class 5 4–6–0s with the flush-sided, curved-top BR1B tender, no. 73078, working from Glasgow's Eastfield shed, on West Highland line duty in March 1961, piloting a Stanier class 5 4–6–0 through Monessie Gorge with the afternoon Fort William–Glasgow train.

for the second phase of that year's Bulleid Pacific crisis on the SR. Following Merchant Navy no. 35020's fracture of a driving axle at speed it was thought prudent to withdraw first the whole of this class for ultrasonic detector examination, then the light Pacifics. To make good the critical power shortage that ensued on the SR's Western Section, Britannia Pacifics and V2 2–6–2s were first borrowed from the WR and ER respectively, to deputise for the Merchant Navy engines, then the class 5s to cover for the light Pacifics. The class 5s were set at one or two front-rank Waterloo–Bournemouth jobs, on which they lost time heavily, but were mostly applied to semi-fast turns on this and the Exeter line during their stay at Nine Elms depot.

By the autumn of that year the WR was clogged with arrears of freight through a shortage of power. That prompted a mass transfer of standard class 5s from LMR sheds to WR depots, principally Shrewsbury, Chester and Bristol St Philips Marsh, to relieve other types for freight haulage. By the end of the year South Wales had its first example with the posting of

Brian Stephenson

21. Ten class 5 4–6–0s destined for the SR's Western Section were paired with the 5,625 gallon, 7 tons capacity BR1F tender otherwise reserved to the class 9 2–10–0s. The SR bestowed ex-'King Arthur' 4–6–0 names on these engines, of which no. 73115, 'King Pellinore', heads the 6.09 pm Waterloo–Basingstoke past Vauxhall on 2 September 1964.

no. 73022 to Swansea Landore, but it was already familiar with the design because from their arrival the Shrewsbury engines had assumed most of the working over the Central Wales line between their home and Swansea. In the following summer, naturally, the WR-based class 5s were added to the ranks of available power for the streams of weekend extra passenger trains to and from Devon and Cornwall.

The only standard class 5s ever sent new from works to the WR were the first ten with Caprotti valve gear, nos. 73125–34, which were delivered to Shrewsbury in the autumn of 1956. However, they were soon moved on to the LMR's Central Division and Shrewsbury was restored the Walschaerts gear engines they had supplanted. But though the WR got all its class 5s secondhand it added some of them to the collection of mixed traffic types which it resolutely decked in the full rig of lined Brunswick green livery during the period of 'Great Western Region' posturing in the second half of the 1950s.

The standard class 5s had not been long on the road before Midland and Scottish crews rated them markedly inferior to the Stanier Black Five. Why this was so – and it was an opinion that went almost everywhere with the BR engines throughout their career – no expert seems to have been able to explain definitively. On test the type performed impressively enough. The initial examination of no. 73008 on the Rugby rollers was not fully satisfying, but when it was replaced by no. 73020, in which the original draughting based on Swindon precepts

22. One of the class 5s which the WR treated to lined green livery, no. 73031: a Bath-based engine for Somerset & Dorset line duty when this photo was taken, it has been appropriated by parent shed Bristol Bath Road for a turn to the north and pauses at Sheffield Midland on the return home with an express from Bradford.

T G Hepburn/Rail Archive Stephenson

had been revised by narrowing the blastpipe orifice, the boiler produced an output vying with the best known of any Black Five. Out on the track between Skipton and Carlisle the standard design sustained an average of 39 mph over the whole, unremitting 17.5 uphill miles from Appleby to Ais Gill summit with the equivalent of 560 tons, simulated by the Mobile Test Units, hanging on its tender.

But somehow all too many drivers found it impossible to repeat this free steaming in day-to-day practice, no matter how the engines were fired (and if they were wrongly fired they seemed to have none of the resilience of a Stanier Black Five). It was not often in their early years that one came across the sort of athleticism displayed by no. 73001 in a Midland run with the 6.33 pm from St Pancras that was reported in 1954. True the 4–6–0 made a run-of-the-mill exit from London with its nine coaches grossing 320 tons, but then the 19.7 miles from Luton to Bedford North were dismissed in just under 15 minutes at an average of 79.1 mph, with a peak of 92 mph just before the Bedford junction. After that, moreover, the class 5 topped the 4 miles of 1 in 119 to Sharnbrook summit at 54 mph.

Many of the best performances to the class 5s' account followed the 1955 arrival of nos. 73080–6 at Stewarts Lane to supersede the ageing class N15 4–6–0s on the SR's Eastern Section (later the SR perpetuated names of these 'King Arthurs', when they went to the scrapheap, on

23. King's Cross shed had some class 5s in 1958: in April that year no. 73157 makes heavy weather of the climb out to Finsbury Park with a down 'Cambridge Buffet Express'.

Brian Morrison

twenty of its class 5s, nos. 73080–9 and 73110–9, the only members of this standard class to be titled during their BR service). Most of the memorable runs on this route were with one of the legendary footplatemen of BR steam's last years at the regulator, Driver Sam Gingell of Stewarts Lane.

On one of these trips Gingell spurred no. 73080 up the 1 in 101 from Herne Hill to such effect with nine coaches grossing 310 tons that he was through Beckenham Junction in a faster time than the recorder had previously logged with any SR electric multiple-unit. On another run, this time coming on eleven coaches of 345 tons gross, Gingell restarted no. 73086 from Chatham and assaulted the five-mile, 1 in 100 Sole Street bank with such brio, regulator wide open and cut-off at 50 per cent, that he actually accelerated from a minimum of 42 to 48 mph on the slope. Then he ripped off the 11.15 miles from Meopham to St Mary Cray at an average of 77 mph, clipping the 94 mph mark at Farningham Road. Before the takeover of the Central Section's Oxted line by diesel-electric multiple-units, the Stewarts Lane class 5s were

T G Hepburn/Rail Archive Stephenson

24. The class 5 4–6–0s came to the GC main line in the closing years of its express service: clearly displaying the original position of the chime whistle behind the chimney on this type, no. 73010 crosses the Midland main line at Loughborough with the York–Bournemouth through train.

also deployed on the heavy morning and evening commuter trains over this difficult route. As for their relatives at neighbouring Nine Elms, these added nothing memorable to the SR's locomotive performance annals.

The ER was evidently thought too satiated with its B1 4–6–0s to need standard class 5s. None was permanently allocated to an ER shed until the start of 1957 when Neasden, then still under the tutelage of King's Cross, received nos. 73155–9 new from Doncaster works. The last three of these, however, were promptly exchanged with Neasden's parent shed for class V2 2–6–2s. Nos. 73157–9 sojourned at King's Cross for most of 1958, but at the end of the year they were shunted on to Sheffield Darnall. While they were at King's Cross – which by the autumn of 1957 was also receiving occasional visits from York-based standard class 5s – the trio was employed mainly on Cambridge and Peterborough semi-fasts, but they also covered that spring's race specials from King's Cross through to Newmarket.

The standard class 5s did eventually preside over the Great Central's express service in its fading months. In the very last week before the curtain was rung down on the Manchester–Marylebone working on 4 January 1960, a later addition to the Neasden stud, no. 73053, came within two seconds of setting a new record for the Nottingham Victoria–Leicester stretch with

25. Caprotti valve gear-fitted class 5 4–6–0 no. 73125 pulls away from Shrewsbury with a Cardiff–Manchester express on 13 August 1956. *Brian Morrison*

a start-to-stop time of 22 minutes 31 seconds for the 23.4 miles on seven coaches grossing 270 tons.

At the start of the 1960s, with the Scottish class 5s' orbit ranging from ex-GSW territory to Aberdeen, Kyle of Lochalsh and (following postings to Eastfield shed) the West Highland, and the allocation of the final dozen 4–6–0s to the NER, the ER was almost the only tract of the system where a sighting of these engines was still worth comment. The NER's first pair, nos. 73160/1, went initially to Blaydon for Carlisle freight hauls previously covered by K1 2–6–0s, but proved outsize for the ex-NER yard's turntable at London Road, Carlisle, and moved on to Gateshead. Others of the NER batch were lodged at York and soon took up regular duty to Lincoln on York–Lowestoft and Yarmouth–York through trains It was not long, however, before East Coast main line dieselisation cascaded the class 5s on to depots in the Leeds Holbeck district such as Normanton and Huddersfield. On the East Coast main line the class 5s seem to have been rather a misfit, with depots undecided whether to apply them to V2 2–6–2 (the equivalent of class 6) or B1 4–6–0 work.

Two class 5s, nos. 73030/1, were outshopped with the embellishment of Westinghouse brakes and a single air compressor on the right-hand side of the smokebox. This provided for their participation along with the two dual-fitted Britannia Pacifics (and, briefly, with a couple of

P B Whitehouse/Colourviews Ltd

26. As built, class 4 4–6–0 no. 75005 at work on the WR's Cambrian lines, pausing at Commins Coch halt.

Westinghouse-fitted ER class L1 2–6–4Ts) in the Midland line test-train evaluation of continuous braking systems for coal trains which were conducted in the early 1950s. At the conclusion of these trials the compressors were removed.

The important and only permanent deviation from basic design in this class was the fitting of Caprotti valve gear to thirty of the forty-seven engines of this type figuring in the 1956 building programme, nos. 73125–54. The decision was prompted by enthusiasm at the performance of the Caprotti gear in the solitary class 8 4–6–2. If the Chief Mechanical Engineer and his aides had had their way these ten class 5s would have been the precursors of a substantial fleet of Caprotti-geared engines, but the BTC vetoed further outlay of time and money on steam technology.

As mentioned earlier, the first Caprotti engines were delivered to the WR shed at Shrewsbury, but nos. 73125–34 soon migrated to the LMR's Patricroft shed. The next ten went new to the Midland's Derby district and the

27. In the mid-1950s some of the WR's class 4 4–6–0s were based at Laira and took a part in South Devon bank pilot duty, as no. 75028 does here, assisting a Castle 4–6–0 up Dainton bank. P B Whitehouse/Colourviews Ltd

75028

Brian Morrison

28. On the Midland the class 4 4–6–0s superseded compound 4–4–0s on the Bedford–St Pancras semi-fasts, one of which no. 75041 scuttles through Elstree on 25 May 1957.

final ten to the Scottish Region, which concentrated them at St Rollox. The LM-based engines came on stage too late for employment that might have exacted running to qualify for honourable mention in the railway press, but on the Glasgow–Aberdeen route the St Rollox ten were pitted against exiled Gresley class A4 Pacifics, with which they shared the express service. And they were not outclassed, either as hill-climbers or as athletes on the flat, where they were timed at almost 90 mph on the 'racecourse' between Coupar Angus and Forfar. Legend has it that a Caprotti class 5 won membership of the 100 mph club in the course of riding tests with a lightweight train under the aegis of BR's test engineers, but I have never seen confirmatory details.

Withdrawal of the standard class 5s began with no. 73027 in 1964 and the type was among the last to be extinguished with the condemnation of no. 73069 in 1968.

In retrospect one has to ask what was gained by undertaking a new class 5 4–6–0 design, apart from achieving some commonality of components with the rest of the standard range, instead of perpetuating the thoroughly proven, versatile and generally respected Stanier Black Five. With the standard class 4 4–6–0 the question is whether it was necessary. It was added to the range in the belief that there were numerous operating specifications that would be better fulfilled by a longer-range, tender version of the class 4 2–6–4 tank. Yet only one of the pre-1948 systems, the Great Western, had felt such a machine to be a justifiable addition to stock. Even then Paddington had not been convinced it needed more than a score of Manor 4–6–0s.

29. The class 4 4–6–0s were one of the several standard classes which were given Somerset & Dorset line experience: on 30 June 1962 no. 75027 of Templecombe shed gives sterling aid to SR rebuilt 'West Country' Pacific no. 34028, 'Eddystone', near Cole on a Liverpool–Bournemouth express.

Derek Cross

The standard class 4 was very much the Derby equivalent of a Manor, with the same 225 lb/sq. in. boiler pressure, 5 ft 8 in. driving wheel diameter and two cylinders of 18 in. diameter, but 28 in. stroke compared with the characteristic 30 in. of the Swindon product. The cardinal distinction was below the running plate, where the BR contoured their engine to fit within the L_1 loading gauge for almost complete route availability, in conjunction with a maximum axle loading of 17¼ tons; total engine weight was 67.9 tons. The dependable boiler of the Stanier/Fairburn LMS 2–6–4 tank was lengthened by 9 in. in the barrel for the 4–6–0 design, for which the parent office was Brighton. All eighty engines of the class were built at Swindon between 1951 and 1957.

For the first fifty of the class 4 4–6–0s the standard tender was the BR2A with inset coal bunker, which had space for 6 tons of coal and 3,500 gallons of water – in the latter instance, not enough to see a 4–6–0 through the Swansea–Shrewsbury run over the Central Wales line on one filling. Central Wales work was one of the first jobs of the 4–6–0s, the first ten of which were handed to the WR, which based most of them at Shrewsbury. The Central Wales duty strengthened scepticism of the need for the design. Previously its passenger trains had been covered principally by ex-LMS Fowler 2–6–4 tanks and Black Five 4–6–0s, the former without much prejudice to schedules through attenuated fuel capacity, the latter without conspicuously knitting brows over axle-loading.

The WR and the LMR shared almost the entire class. In the first half of the 1950s the WR scattered its allocation throughout the Region. By 1955 the most prominent – because they

S C Nash

30. The SR-based class 4 4–6–0s had the flush-sided BR1B tender and were modified with double chimneys: no. 75068 was an example, here leaving Hastings with the summer 10.20 am to Sheffield on 27 July 1963.

worked in such a photogenic environment – were the examples ranging over the Cambrian system from Oswestry shed and serving as pilots over the South Devon banks from Plymouth Laira; others were at Oxford and Cardiff Canton primarily for secondary main line passenger jobs. At that time the LMR's class 4s were mostly congregated in the Chester motive power district; small clusters were to be found at Southport, Bedford, Accrington and Bletchley, where in all cases they took over passenger jobs that seemed previously to have been well within the operational competence of 2–6–4 tanks.

It was a class 4–6–0 which in the summer of 1957 heralded some change of mind on the draughting arrangements of the standard types. As a preceding chapter has indicated, the Railway Executive team originally envisaged the

31. The first few class 4 2–6–0s went to Motherwell shed and no. 76001 was still wearing a Motherwell shedplate when it was encountered far away on 13 August 1960, leaving Mallaig with a West Highland train for Glasgow.

D M C Hepburne-Scott/Rail Archive Stephenson

standardisation of double blastpipes and chimneys on all the larger types in the range. But the concluding stages of the design were influenced by the findings of Swindon's refined test procedures under S.O.Ell, which suggested that scientific shaping and sizing of a single chimney could have a more dramatic effect on continuous steaming propensity than arbitrary resort to a double blastpipe and chimney in subservience to fashion. Despite the fact that the BTC test routines to which no. 75006 was submitted at the start of 1952 on the Swindon rollers and, as usual, on the WR main line with loads of up to sixteen bogies, had marked it with the lowest boiler efficiency of any standard type examined this way, the class was left unaltered until the deteriorating quality of coal nagged BR's traction chiefs more persistently in the later 1950s.

Then no. 75029 was modified at Swindon with a double blastpipe and chimney – in this first instance some oversight allowed Swindon to get away with the fitting of its own pattern, which was a rather monstrous excrescence on the squat front end of the class 4's boiler. On test

Derek Cross

32. The ex-GSW system was another Scottish hunting ground of the class 4 2–6–0s: Ayr-based no. 76097 leaves its home town with a Kilmarnock local on 22 June 1963.

with less than prime quality coal the revamped 4–6–0 steamed continuously at a rate well in excess of that recorded in the 1952 trials, and over 50 per cent higher than the norm for a class 4 4–6–0 in traffic. Moreover, it was said to have dealt comfortably with some fast main line work normally rostered for class 5 power.

From this stemmed the decision to experiment with a double blastpipe and chimney on a 2–10–0 (no. 92178) and a proclaimed intention to fit all eighty class 4s with double chimneys, but in the event only the SR's final fifteen of the class, and a few of the WR's stud were retrospectively modified. The initial double-chimney class 4 no. 75029, incidentally, was one of those the WR graced with fully lined passenger green livery during its years of dedication to imprinting the nearest thing to the old GWR livery on as much of its steam locomotive stock as could claim relevance to passenger employment.

The last twenty class 4 4–6–0s, nos. 75050–79 (ten more had been programmed for allocation to the ER but were cancelled in the shadow of dieselisation), were paired with bigger, flush-sided BR1B tenders affording 7 tons coal and 4,725 gallons water capacity. Just why the Railway Executive team opted for such comparatively puny tenders for the first series of standard engines has never been convincingly

33. One of Leicester Midland's class 4 2–6–0s, no. 76086, bustles past Long Eaton Junction with a Nottingham–Chesterfield train in the late 1950s.

T G Hepburn/Rail Archive Stephenson

explained. The inset coal bunker's asset of creating channels of rearward vision is obvious, but only for signal sighting; it did little to improve enginemen's appreciation of distance when they were backing on to a train. Considering that neither LMS high-sided tenders nor the even bulkier LNER eight-wheelers had been a bone of contention with enginemen, one wonders why it was thought worthwhile forfeiting capacity in the first BR standard tenders. Surely no one visualised the Britannia Pacifics being frequently rostered to tender-first working. Granted, the inset coal bunker was a familiar feature of many latter-day tender designs on the European mainland, but these were not so limited in length as the BR tenders had to be to fit the majority of turntables (as it was the Liverpool Street turntable had to be lengthened before it could accept a Britannia). The BR designers sensibly switched to flush-sided tenders when it became apparent that the inset coal bunker was not regarded by enginemen as their biggest blessing since colour-light signals, and as the standard locomotives were programmed for work demanding increased fuel capacity.

The second of these factors was obviously paramount in the arrangement of engines for the SR, with its lack of water troughs, and it was the SR which took the last fifteen of the class 4s. The first five went to the Eastern Section's Dover shed, which used them on important London jobs such as the 8.59 am to Charing Cross and 9.20 am to Victoria, a non-stop from Canterbury East to Chatham and otherwise either a Bulleid Pacific or a Schools 4–4–0 duty. The remaining ten went first to the Western Section's Exmouth Junction depot and launched their career on the SR routes west of Exeter, chiefly the Okehampton–Plymouth line. Before the end of the decade, however, these ten were dispersed, some to the Somerset & Dorset line, a couple to the Central Section and four to Basingstoke. After the Kent Coast electrification the Eastern Section's class 4s were added to the Brighton, Three Bridges and Basingstoke allocations.

On none of the services with which they were most consistently associated did the standard class 4 4–6–0s leave a memorable imprint. On the Bedford–St Pancras semi-fasts the BR engines, with their modern front-end layout and servicing aids such as self-cleaning smokebox, rocking grate and self-emptying ashpan, were clearly superior mechanisms to the decrepit ex-Midland compound 4–4–0s which they relieved, but the common consensus rated them if anything less competent in timing these trains. On the short-haul Lancashire passenger jobs and the Bletchley–Euston commuter trains they were certainly not preferred to a 2–6–4 tank. In his book *Living With London Midland Locomotives* (Ian Allan, 1977) A. J. Powell described how Southport shed, distraught with the capricious steaming of its quintet of class 4s and the withering fire that they drew from the local operators, borrowed the newly modified double-chimney no. 75029 on loan from Oxford to see if the front-end change had solved the problem. But even this engine could not be coaxed up to 70 mph on near-level track, moderately loaded with seven bogies, without boiler pressure slumping well below 175 lb/sq. in. and the water almost disappearing from the gauge glass. 'It was returned to Oxford,' concluded Powell, 'quite unmourned.'

First of the class to be condemned, in 1964, was no. 75067 and the type's career with BR ended in 1968 with the withdrawal of no. 75048.

Examples preserved:

Class 5 4–6–0 nos.

73050	Nene Valley Railway
73082	Bluebell Railway
73129	Midland Railway Trust, Butterley

Class 4 4–6–0 nos.

75027	Bluebell Railway
75029	East Somerset Railway
75069	Severn Valley Railway
75078	Keighley & Worth Valley Railway

6
The Moguls

In 1947 H. G. Ivatt had presided over the design of a very competent modern successor to the traditional British all-purpose machine for secondary chores, the 0–6–0. BR's motive power inheritance included battalions of 0–6–0s, many of them at pensionable age, so a standardised version of the Ivatt class 4 2–6–0 was another uncontroversial addition to the BR range. In 17½ in. by 26 in. cylinder size, 225 lb/sq. in. boiler pressure, even in engine wheelbase and total length over buffers the Ivatt and standard types were twins; but the BR design had the edge in looks, thanks to a drop plate descending from running plate to buffer beam that eliminated the stark front-end angularity of the LMS machine. The BR class 4's front-end also had the advantage of a blastpipe and chimney proportioned in the light of Swindon's successful experiments with one of the Ivatt engines.

Doncaster was the parent office for the class 4 design, of which 115 examples were built between 1952 and 1957. Nos. 76000–19 and 76075–99 were assembled at Horwich, the remainder at Doncaster. The type was launched with the inset coal bunker Type BR2A tender holding 6 tons of coal and 3,500 gallons of water, but nos. 76053–69 for the SR were paired with the flush-sided BR1B of 7 tons and 4,725 gallons capacity.

Doncaster and Horwich finished their first class 4 2–6–0s almost simultaneously at the end of 1952, the first five Horwich engines going to Motherwell, the inaugural Doncaster engines to the NER. Nos. 76005–19 went to the SR, which shedded them at Eastleigh, there to open the operational account for which the type is perhaps most respectfully remembered. Not for them merely the humdrum work with which one associated most of their 0–6–0 forebears (with the possible exception of the LNER class J39s working the Great Eastern line), but also some quite onerous cross-country express passenger haulage. In their very first summer at Eastleigh, after bedding down on stopping passenger jobs that included turns to Reading and via the then ex-DN&S line to Didcot, the class 4 2–6–0s were deputed not only to the Brighton–Bournemouth through trains, but also to the haulage to and from Salisbury of the expresses linking South Wales with the Wessex coast, some of which aggregated twelve bogies. On the descent from Salisbury to Romsey, moreover, the 2–6–0s could accelerate smoothly to the 70 mph mark and more.

Once or twice the Eastleigh 2–6–0s were commandeered by Salisbury depot for stopping or summer extra passenger turns to Exeter, and in the spring of 1956 the permanent allocation of some of the 2–6–0s to Exmouth Junction

34. Class 4 2–6–0 no. 76061, one of the SR's allocation with type BR1B flush-sided tenders, on the cross-country route which tested them most: the Redhill-based engine is threading the Surrey hills near Albury, en route from Reading to Tonbridge with a Birkenhead–Ramsgate/Margate through train on 18 June 1956.

R T M Bicknell

seemed a possibility, as the class 4 4–6–0s were said to be overlong for some tasks west of Exeter; however, Salisbury was eventually the most westerly outpost of the class on the West of England main line. The high-capacity tender batch spent the 1950s at Redhill shed, whence they too were taxed with the haulage of very well-loaded cross-country expresses on the line from Redhill in the summer, but at the end of the decade they were added to the Western Section stud.

Elsewhere the class 4 2–6–0s did little to attract attention or for that matter displeasure. The NER was allocated nos. 76020–4, then nos. 76045–52, fresh from works, and so long as it operated engines of the type deployed them chiefly in the Darlington and Gateshead motive power districts. The ER was assigned nos. 76030–44, which it shared initially between

Derek Cross

35. The NER's class 3 2–6–0s started their career on the now vanished trans-Pennine route over Stainmore summit between Tees-side and the West Coast main line: here no. 77002 pilots Ivatt class 4 2–6–0 no. 43029 into Tebay with a Newcastle–Blackpool train in July 1961.

Stratford and Neasden depots, later moving the Stratford batch briefly to March ahead of the GE line's dieselisation and suburban electrification before yielding them to the SR's Brighton shed in 1962. The LMR took nos. 76075–89 from the Horwich assembly line and deployed them in the north-west. The remainder were all for the Scottish Region, which distributed them throughout its fief from Stranraer to Kittybrewster.

Except that the Neasden engines were transferred to Cricklewood in 1962, and that in the same year Stoke gained some of the class 4s, this broadly summarises the class 4 2–6–0s' working life. The scrapyards started to take their toll with no. 76028 in 1964 and gathered in the last working example, no. 76084, in 1967.

S C Nash

36. Some class 3 2–6–0s gravitated to the SR in the 1960s: no. 77014 mounts Upwey bank with the 4.46 pm Weymouth–Bournemouth on 18 May 1967.

The class 3 2–6–0s' inclusion in the standard range was motivated by the continued existence in the immediate post-war years of some lines limited to a 16-ton axle loading, which proscribed class 4 power. With the advantage of hindsight one finds it baffling that either the civil engineers' resources or their technology were apparently thought incapable of eradicating these handicaps before pre-nationalisation locomotives that met the weight restrictions had fallen into unrepairable bits. As it was, the class 3 2–6–0 was not committed to production until the second half of 1953.

Nos. 77000–19 emerged from Swindon the following year, to be shared between the North Eastern and Scottish Regions – and that was the sum total of the class. The civil engineers or the intrusion of diesel railcars had nullified the case for any more. Given the shortness of its production run and of its career the class 3 2–6–0 must have been ton for ton one of the most costly types in the whole BR standard locomotive programme.

Dimensionally the class 4 2–6–0 boiler would have fitted into the class 3 layout, but it would have overweighted the lower powered 2–6–0. With no other Derby-derived boiler suitable for the class 3 on file, the Riddles team opted for an adaptation of the Swindon no. 2 boiler used in the GWR 51XX and 81XX 2–6–2 tanks and the 56XX 0–6–2 tanks – perhaps needless to say, topping it with a dome amongst other modifications. The same boiler, identically revised, was applied to the standard class 3 2–6–2 tank, which had many other features in

37. One of Millhouses shed's class 2 2–6–0s, no. 78025, eases the 2.30 pm Nottingham Midland–Chesterfield local round the Long Eaton Junction curve on 9 May 1955.

T G Hepburn/Rail Archive Stephenson

common with the tender engine, such as its two $17\frac{1}{2}$ in. by 26 in. cylinders and 5 ft 3 in. driving wheels. The 57 ton 2–6–0 was paired with the BR2A tender, holding 6 tons of coal and 3,500 gallons of water.

The NER's half of the class, nos. 77000–4/10–14, spent most of their life at depots in the Darlington motive power district, catching the lens of photographers mostly when they were given a share of work over the trans-Pennine line from Darlington to Tebay in the 1960s. However, York, Hull Dairycoates and Scarborough each housed one of the class. The Scottish engines' life centred mostly on work from

Derek Cross

38. The Cambrian was one WR arena of class 2 2–6–0 operation: no. 78007 from Machynlleth shed accelerates a Pwlhelli–Aberystwyth train away from Barmouth on 11 August 1960.

Hamilton and Hurlford depots. The class survived intact until 1965 and the last survivor, no. 77014, was dismissed in 1967.

Like the BR standard class 2 2–6–2 tank, the standard class 2 2–6–0 was essentially the successful Ivatt LMS engine of the same wheel arrangement marginally revised to embody standard components and, of course, to carry the standard cab. Such detail as boiler, cylinders, driving wheel diameter and wheelbase was a replica of the 1952 LMS design's make-up. Derby had the responsibility for the design, which was completed with the BR3 tender of 4 tons coal and 3,000 gallons water capacity.

The entire class of sixty-five engines was built at Darlington between 1952 and 1956. The WR took the first ten, nos. 78000–9, and put them to work on the Cambrian system from Oswestry and Machynlleth; it also gave some of them green livery. The NER took in nos. 78000–19 at West Auckland and this was another standard class that patrolled the Darlington–Penrith/

Tebay route for most of the later 1950s; when that was shut down some of this batch were passed on to the LMR, which was assigned nos. 78020–44/55–64 when they were new and dispersed them fairly widely.

The rest were Scottish Region servants; the sheds where they had the longest tenancy were Motherwell and Hawick, on the ill-fated Waverley route from Edinburgh to Carlisle. During 1962, when some of the LMR lot were under ER command in the Sheffield district, nos. 78020–2 were briefly on the Doncaster depot roster. The class went to the breakers between 1963 and 1967.

Examples preserved:
Class 4 2–6–0 nos
76017 Mid-Hants Railway
76079 Steamport, Southport

Class 2 2–6–0 nos.
78018 Market Bosworth Light Railway
78019 Severn Valley Railway
78022 Keighley & Worth Valley Railway

7
The Tank Engines

The 2–6–4 tank was almost as valuable an LMS contribution to the standard armoury of British steam in the latter's last three decades as the Black Five 4–6–0. BR categorised it as a mixed traffic engine, but its versatility was limited for most practical purposes to hard slogging with heavy, multi-stop commuter trains on the one hand, and on the other a zest for 75–80 mph when it was given the gun on non-stop, short haul express turns within the 50–60 miles' range of its side-tank capacity. The LMS sensibly classified it 4P, since the 2–6–4's usefulness as a freight hauler was vitiated by the fluctuating value of its adhesion weight, depending as it did on the weight of supplies in tanks and bunker; and also because of a tank engine's lack of tender brakes as an additional restraint in years when the majority of British freight wagons lacked continuous brake.

From the Fowler design of 1927 through Stanier's two and three-cylinder types to Fairburn's final LMS version, with its shortened wheelbase for wider route availability and self-cleaning smokebox, cutaway front-end framing and other detail refinements devised for easier, cheaper maintenance, the LMS 2–6–4 tanks had all been conspicuously successful. For every job it undertook the self-contained machine was obviously less expensive to maintain as well as to buy than a tender locomotive, apart from the operational economy of engines that did not need to be turned at terminals (though in many areas enginemen strove to get them turned between trips for the superior comfort of driving chimney first – some would even forfeit their own rest period to get it done). Given the number of shorter-distance passenger jobs up and down the country still performed in the early 1950s by tender engines of questionable suitability but generally patent age, further production of 2–6–4 tanks was one item at least of the standard locomotive programme that no one queried.

The Fairburn 2–6–4 tank production line had been kept rolling under the nationalised regime, and at first the Riddles team was disposed to let this design serve BR unaltered. But second thoughts dictated its revision to conform with the newly-formulated BR L_1 loading gauge for virtually unrestricted route availability. Brighton was entrusted with the design, with the obvious consequence that the latter had a number of components in common with that of the standard class 4 2–6–0, for which Brighton was also the parent office. Apart from the first ten, nos. 80000–9 and five more, nos. 80054–8, which were erected at Derby, and nos. 80106–15, which were Doncaster products of 1954, the entire class of 155 BR standard class 4 2–6–4 tanks was built at Brighton works; the final

Brian Morrison

39. One of the first jobs for the class 4 2–6–4Ts was the Euston outer suburban service of the LMR: no. 80039 makes for Watford Tunnel with a Tring train on 9 August 1952.

40. The ex-LMS suburban lines radiating from Glasgow were a familiar class 4 2–6–4T workplace: this pair, nos. 80052 and 80030, are double-heading a special past Upper Port Glasgow on the Kilmacolm line on 6 July 1963.

Derek Cross

engine was in fact the last locomotive constructed at Brighton. Production spanned the period from 1951 to 1956.

Satisfaction of the L_1 parameters exacted a substantial reduction of the Fairburn tank's cylinder diameter from 19⅝ in. to 18 in. (but stroke was lengthened from 26 to 28 in.) and to offset this boiler pressure was advanced from 200 to 225 lb so as to secure almost the same nominal tractive effort. In all essential dimensions the boiler was the same as that of the LM engine, but differently manufactured for commonality with the rest of the BR range. One more noticeable change was the reduction of driving wheel diameter from 5 ft 9 in. to 5 ft 8 in. Although there was no resultant con-

41. One of the SR Central Section's class 4 2–6–4Ts, no. 80032 of Brighton, on the Cuckoo Line near Rotherfield with a Tunbridge Wells–Eastbourne train in March 1960. *Derek Cross*

traction of the Fairburn engine's 15 ft 4 in. driving wheelbase, the standard design was almost 2½ ft shorter in length over buffers; and although the latter, at 86 tons 13 cwt, was almost a ton lighter, its 53 tons 1 cwt of adhesion weight was nearly 1½ tons more than that of the LM engine.

Nationalisation had already bestowed some Fairburn 2–6–4 tanks on the SR. One of the earliest motive power experiments ordained by the Railway Executive was the evaluation of a couple of LM engines, the then newly-built nos. 42198/9, as successors to the assortment of elderly machines maintaining that Region's unelectrified secondary passenger services. The pair was put to the proof chiefly on the Central Section, but also invited to show its mettle on Eastern Section workings that included non-stop runs between Ashford and Victoria, where no. 42199 was timed at 85 mph on at least one journey. (Inexplicably, the SR mobilised one of its class W 2–6–4 tanks, a type specifically created for heavy freight transfer work, to run the same course as a bench-mark – a predictably pointless exercise that had the quite unsuitable Maunsell engine overheated as soon as it was asked for speed.) As a result of this spring 1948

42. Some of the class 4 2–6–4Ts' most exacting work was on the Tilbury line: no. 80097 sets off from Southend Central with a midday Shoeburyness–Fenchurch Street train on 6 September 1959.

S Rickard

trial Brighton works was commissioned to build forty-one new Fairburn 2–6–4 tanks for the SR.

Brighton was first to finish a batch of the new standard class 4 2–6–4 tanks and its initial ten, nos. 80010–9, were assigned to Tunbridge Wells West depot in the summer and autumn of 1951. The benefit of the standard type's more compact outline was immediately apparent in its freedom to traverse the notoriously tight-to-gauge section between Grove Junction, Tunbridge Wells, and Tonbridge, which was denied to the Fairburn engines. During the years the Fairburn and standard designs worked shoulder to shoulder on the Tunbridge Wells services, the distinction made quite a cat's-cradle of the locomotive rostering and not infrequently enforced a last minute switch of engines when a Fairburn 2–6–4 tank was found to have been allocated to a trip over the restricted section. Why the seemingly obvious course of congregating more of the standard type on the SR and shipping the Region's Fairburn engines to north of the Thames to join their relations on the LMR was not pursued until the end of the 1950s, is unfathomable.

Derby works did not get round to assembling the numerical first ten of the last batch until mid-1952, by which time Brighton's output was in the 80040s. The first Derby examples, and the second batch, nos. 80020–30 from Brighton, introduced the type to Scotland, where it established a secure foothold on the

M Mitchell

43. One of Leeds Neville Hill's class 4 2–6–4Ts, no. 80118, is ennobled on 20 December 1959 with charge of the 'Harrogate Sunday Pullman', which it is working on from Leeds to destination.

passenger turns from Glasgow to Lanarkshire and the Clyde coast, working from Polmadie and Corkerhill sheds, and on the former Great North of Scotland line local jobs from Aberdeen, operating out of Kittybrewster depot. On the Glasgow St Enoch–Ayr trains, with the temptation of non-stop runs of 35 miles from the start to Troon, the standard engines were soon demonstrating an 80 mph capability akin to that of the Fairburn engines on the gentle slope beyond Beith. But in another respect they prompted unfavourable comparison with their predecessors; a penalty had to be paid for their slimming within the L_1 loading gauge in the irritating fore-and-aft motion their longer piston stroke imparted to the train and its passengers when they were being put to the spur.

The LMR was next in line for deliveries. Here the engines settled down in three main spheres of activity in the mid-1950s: both the Euston and the St Pancras outer suburban services, which the newcomers operated from Watford, Bletchley and Kentish Town sheds; and in Lancashire, from bases at Newton Heath and Bury. By and large LMR enginemen seem to have found the standard engines acceptable, if not the equal of their LM forebears.

Derek Cross

44. No. 80135, one of the Tilbury Line class 4 2–6–4Ts exiled by electrification, ends up on the Cambrian line in June 1964, attacking the climb to Talerdigg summit with an Aberystwyth–Oswestry train.

The hardest regular graft asked of the class was probably the lot of the Eastern Region's batch, nos. 80069–80/96–80105/31–6, which worked the London Tilbury & Southend line until the latter's electrification at the start of the 1960s. Here the standard engines were daily grappling with packed commuter trains of well over 300 tons over a road that included the pronounced gable of Laindon bank, inclined at 1 in 110 for more than a mile of its western ramp, and sloped mostly at 1 in 110–132 on the longer eastern side. Yet more than once the drivers of Southend-bound trains were timed to take their 2–6–4s storming up the hill from West Horndon to the summit on full regulator at an average of almost 60 mph.

Following the LTS electrification the line's standard 2–6–4 tanks were dispersed far and wide. A couple, nos. 80130/37, had been given a brief spell on King's Cross outer suburban services in the autumn of 1958, but subsequent dieselisation had closed doors there. So after a few of the displaced engines had paused briefly on Stratford's establishment, the majority were

45. After the takeover of SR Oxted line services by dmu's its class 4 2–6–4Ts gravitated to the south-west: no. 80147 helps class 'MN' 4–6–2 no. 35011, 'General Steam Navigation', up the hill from Weymouth past Upwey Wishing Well Halt with a Waterloo express on 20 July 1963.

handed to the WR, which posted them predominantly in the Shrewsbury district, though a handful were dispatched to Swansea East Dock for Central Wales line passenger duty.

The North Eastern Region's turn for an allocation of the engines did not come until the summer of 1955, when nos. 80116–20 were sent new from Brighton to Whitby, but following the 1958 abandonment of passenger service on the coast line thence to Scarborough, they were removed to Leeds Neville Hill. A number of the redundant LTS standard 2–6–4 tanks were reassigned to the NER, which found them a home at Ardsley.

The last tract of BR to see these engines fresh from works was the London area of the Great Central, with the delivery to Neasden shed in the 1956 summer of nos. 80137–44 to relieve L1 2–6–4 tanks (needed to make a better fist of empty stock working up the bank out of King's Cross than 0–6–2 tanks) on the Marylebone suburban services. Brighton's final batch, nos. 80145–54, were sent no further than the local shed to supplement the SR Central Section's stud of the class.

The exchange of the thirty-four Brighton-built Fairburn tanks remaining on the SR for an equivalent number of the BR standard model from LMR depots was finally ordered at the end of 1960. The reason circulated at the time was that the Fairburn engines were easier to fit with the BR standard AWS gear (the SR was at the end of the queue for AWS installation, partly because of problems in safeguarding the apparatus from interference by third-rail traction current, partly because SR operators themselves

46. In the later 1950s the majority of the SR's class 3 2–6–2Ts were housed at Exmouth Junction for South Devon branch work: here no. 82017 leaves Woodbury Road with the 4.25 pm Exeter Central–Exmouth on 16 June 1958.

fretted that drivers cruising through a close sequence of double-yellow aspects in the suburban peak would soon become insensitive to the accompanying warnings). In time, nevertheless, standard class 4 2–6–4s operating in BR AWS territory were fitted to work with the device.

The influx of standard 2–6–4 tanks ensuing from this deal introduced the type to SR Eastern Section sheds at Stewarts Lane, Ashford and Dover. But completion of the Kent Coast electrification was only a year and a half away, and with that the majority of the ousted standard tanks were transferred to the Western Section. Some went to Eastleigh, whence they ranged as far as Bath over the Somerset & Dorset (later in the 1960s WR-based 2–6–4 tanks also worked the S&D) and Weymouth, in the latter case proving a valuable operating standby when the Weymouth turntable was out of commission. However, most of the incoming standard 2–6–4s were assembled at Exmouth Junction to take over the Exmouth branch and secondary main line passenger jobs on both sides of Exeter. On the branch jobs they supplanted the BR standard class 3 2–6–2 tank, never a very popular machine in the West Country.

Apart from the 1962 switch of some Polmadie engines to St Margarets shed for secondary passenger work out of Edinburgh Waverley as a result of Glasgow's 'Blue Train' electrification, that was the last newsworthy redistribution of

47. The WR's freedom with lined green livery extended even to some of its class 3 2–6–2Ts, among them no. 82009, photographed near Llwyngwril with a Barmouth–Dovey Junction train on 19 April 1963.

C M C Hepburne-Scott/Rail Archive Stephenson

the standard 2–6–4 tanks. The surge of WR dieselisation and the concomitant slaughter of its steam power in 1962 had the first of the class, no. 80103 of the WR's allocation, withdrawn that year, but it was 1967 before the 2–6–4 tanks were obliterated from BR's working stock with the condemnation of no. 80152. But this has been a highly favoured class for preservation, with as many as nine surviving in private hands.

The forty-five class 3 2–6–2 tanks, the motivation for which was outlined in the preceding chapter, were designed and built at Swindon between 1952 and 1955. This type's two 17½ in. by 26 in. cylinders and 5 ft 3 in. driving wheels were identical in dimension with those of its possible – but uninspiring – model, the Stanier class 3 2–6–2 tank, but though the BR machine had a more compact 15 ft 4 in. driving wheelbase compared with the LMS engine's

48. The SR class 3 2–6–2Ts expelled from Devon by diesel multiple-units ended up at Nine Elms displacing class M7 0–4–4Ts on such Waterloo empty stock workings as the 'Bournemouth Belle', the cars of which are brought into Clapham yard in 1963 by no. 82017.

Brian Stephenson

16 ft 6 in., the standard type scaled 74 tons 1 cwt, compared with the Stanier type's 71 ft 5 cwt. The boilers of both were pressed at 200 lb/sq. in.

The WR took the first ten of the class and initially based them at Tyseley as power for the Stratford-on-Avon local trains. Incoming diesel multiple-units soon made them superfluous in the West Midlands and they moved on briefly to sheds further north-west, such as Wellington, Chester and Wrexham. Next, after a fairly exhaustive preliminary trial the majority of this first batch was reunited and transferred to Barry and Treherbert to augment the South Wales resources of ex-GW 2–6–2 tanks for the 1953–4 winter launch of an intensified and comprehensively revised regular-interval passenger service in the Cardiff valleys.

The one significant complaint voiced about the class 3 standard tanks was that their coal bunker capacity was undersized for through running from Barry to Treherbert. That was silenced by reshaping the interior of the bunker in the second WR batch, nos. 82030–44, to raise its capacity from 3 tons to 3¾ tons, though Barry firemen protested that the new profile of the bunker floor made their work more exhausting.

With the mid-1955 delivery of this series to South Wales the pioneer engines were mostly shipped to Newton Abbot to divide their time between Dainton banking duty and stopping passenger haulage to Exeter and on the Kingswear branch in South Devon's remaining years of steam power. The last operational spheres of

49. Auto-fitted class 2 2–6–2T no. 84007 heads the Seaton Junction–Stamford push-pull under the Kettering–Saxby line of the LMR.

T G Hepburn/Rail Archive Stephenson

the WR engines were principally the Bristol district (where one or two were posted to local work on the Somerset & Dorset amongst other chores); Taunton branch work; and the Cambrian system, where Machynlleth was operating ten of the class 3s in the summer of 1962. The WR treated a number of the engines to green livery, at first unlined but eventually in some cases in the full panoply of express passenger lined green.

The SR's class 3s, nos. 82010–9/22–25, spent most of their career shared between Eastleigh and Exmouth Junction sheds. At the latter, as recorded earlier, they were in time supplanted by standard class 4 tanks. That move reflected the progressive uplift of track standards by the civil engineers which steadily licensed more of the system for heavier engines and curtailed the operating need of class 3s. At the close of 1962 the SR assembled its allocation in the London area, for the most part at Nine Elms to trundle empty stock to and from Waterloo, but in one or two cases for short interludes of trip freight working from Feltham shed.

Coupled with the heavy ordering of diesel multiple-units the outcome was the cancellation of 1954 plans for a further eighteen class 3s, ten for the WR and the remainder for the NER. So the NER's acquaintance with the class 3s was limited to just four engines, nos. 82026–9, which started life on the doomed Darlington–Barnard Castle–Penrith/Tebay cross-country route from Darlington and Kirkby Stephen sheds, then moved on to Malton and Scarborough. Withdrawals were initiated in 1964 and by 1967 the class was extinct with the condemnation of the last survivor, no. 82029.

Little needs to be said of the standard class 2 2–6–2 tank, which as expected was a modest revamping of the competent Ivatt 2–6–2 tank of the LMS to employ the maximum of standard BR fitments. In view of this kinship Derby was the natural parent office for the design, which materialised as thirty engines: nos. 84000–19 for the LMR, built at Crewe in 1953; and then, three years later than their original slot in the building programme, nos. 84020–9, erected at Darlington, for the SR in 1957. The class at first had the vacuum control gear for push-pull operation as a standard attachment, but this was removed as push-pull workings were eliminated either by the advent of diesel railcars or by service closures.

In their time on the SR the class 2s were based in Kent, at Ashford and Ramsgate, but following the Kent Coast electrification all thirty engines were concentrated on the LMR, apart from a brief 1962 stint by no. 84009 at Hull Dairycoates. The LMR dispersed them throughout its territory, from Kentish Town and Bletchley to Fleetwood and Bolton. No. 84012 was the first to be condemned, in 1963, and no. 84028 the last, in 1965.

Hopes of a longer life, both for these engines and for steam working in the Isle of Wight, crumbled when a 1961 proposal to appoint them successors to the island's senescent class 02 0–4–4 tanks was defeated by the prospective bill for adapting the Ryde workshops to maintain their greater bulk.

Examples preserved:

Class 4 2–6–4T nos.

80002	Keighley & Worth Valley Railway
80064	Dart Valley Railway
80078	Swanage Railway
80079	Severn Valley Railway
80080	Peak Railway Society
80100	Bluebell Railway
80105	Scottish Preservation Society, Falkirk
80135	North Yorkshire Moors Railway
80136	North Staffordshire Railway Society
80151	Chappel Steam Centre

8

The Class 9 2–10–0s

One of the two thoroughly successful types in the BR standard range did not figure in the first draft construction programme compiled for Riddles' endorsement. That propounded a 2–8–2 as the heavy freight engine in the range when one was needed – which was not immediately, for BR's stock of modern 2–8–0s had just been substantially augmented by droves of Stanier and Riddles WD 2–8–0s returned from the war. A 2–8–2 rather than a fresh 2–8–0 design was advocated to raise heavy freight engine power output and speed potential. The first sketch envisaged a 5 ft 3 in. driving-wheel machine that would employ the same chassis and double-chimney boiler as the mixed traffic variant of the two class 7 4–6–2 types originally suggested.

However, the indulgence of two class 7 Pacific studs, one a specifically express passenger type with a 275 lb/sq. in. boiler and 6 ft 6 in. drivers, the other a more versatile machine with a 225 lb/sq. in. boiler and 6 ft drivers, was forgone when comparative tests of East Coast 6 ft 8 in. A1 and 6 ft 2 in. A2 Pacifics reinforced Bulleid Pacific evidence that a 6 in. difference in driving wheel diameter was immaterial to speed potential in powerful locomotives with scientifically-designed steam passages. The class 7 4–6–2 was reshaped as the all-purpose Britannia. And thereupon the 2–8–2 was redesigned with a Britannia boiler and as many other class 7 components as possible.

But Riddles, armed with the record of his WD 2–10–0s, pressed the case for a ten-coupled engine's superior adhesion – a factor in which the outline 2–8–2 showed little advance over a 2–8–0. Although at least one analytical exercise suggested that whatever advantage a 2–10–0 gained in starting would be lost at around the 35 mph mark, so that on a brake-fitted merchandise freight a 2–8–2 would be first past the post, once Riddles was satisfied that a wide-firebox 2–10–0 with 5 ft driving wheels could be compressed within BR's L_2 loading gauge – which would give it near-total main line availability – he voted for it.

The decision forfeited standardisation in the freight engine of any significant components from the rest of the range apart from cab and tender, and enforced some tricky shaping of boiler, firegrate and ashpan. The barrel of the 250 lb/sq. in. boiler was 4½ in. smaller at the rear end than a Britannia's because of its high pitch, and the 2–10–0's firegrate had to be humped and slightly reduced in area. The two 20 in. by 28 in. cylinders exhausted to a single chimney in the first batches of the class 9, but in 1957 the first of the second lot of 2–10–0s to be erected at Swindon, no. 92178, was turned out with a double blastpipe and chimney. The

50. Class 9 2–10–0 no. 92013 on the stationary test plant at Rugby in the course of its BTC performance and efficiency evaluation.

Cecil J Allen Collection

superior output and coal economy it demonstrated under Swindon's test routines led to standardisation of the arrangement for further construction. In all, eighty of the eventual 251 2–10–0s had double chimneys, but of these four only – nos. 92000/1/6 and 92079 – were conversions from single-chimney originals. Incidentally, Riddles had specified that the class 9 be topped by the rather puny chimney of his WD 2–10–0, but for unknown reasons his order was not followed; by the time the first class 9s were into production Riddles had retired, so the indiscipline went unremarked – mercifully, so far as the look of BR 2–10–0s was concerned, whatever compliance might or might not have done for the engines' efficiency.

The class 9 2–10–0s were the last of the BR standard types to be ordered. Although the start of dieselisation was proclaimed within a year of the assembly line's inauguration in 1954, construction of the eleven batches of 2–10–0s was spread over the rest of the decade. Not until 1960 was it brought to an end with a formal dedication before a large audience at Swindon works of the last steam locomotive to be built for BR, no. 92220, 'Evening Star', to the

51. The ER was the first Region to put the class 9 2–10–0s to regular fast brake-fitted freight work: no. 92140 of New England shed is storming northward through Hadley Wood.

Derek Cross

specially ceded lined green passenger livery to which Swindon had added the Swindon hallmark of a copper-capped chimney. Swindon was entrusted with three lots of the 2–10–0s, nos. 92087–96, 92178–92202 and 92203–92220. The remainder were all built at Crewe, which terminated its steam construction with no. 92250 in December 1958. The 2–10–0s operated with four standard types of tender, BR1B, BR1C, BR1F and BR1G, none of them unique to the class, and the choice of which depended chiefly on Regional assignment, and one specialised model, the BR1K, of which more shortly. The parent office for the 2–10–0 design was Brighton.

The Western Region was handed the first seven 2–10–0s for operation from Ebbw Junction early in 1954, but got no more newly-minted until 1959. All new production in the intervening years was for the East Coast Regions and the LMR. None were allocated new to the Southern and Scottish Regions, though both had subsequent experience of the type.

A weakness that had the first 2–10–0s in trouble within days of their arrival at Ebbw Junction was a new design of regulator, operated by external rodding as on the Pacifics, that took the form of a sliding grid throttle in the

52. Class 9 2–10–0s assigned to the NER's Tyne Dock–Consett iron ore haul were fitted with a pair of compressors – seen mounted mid-frame on no. 92062 – to operate the wagons' air-powered discharge doors. No. 92062 has the BR1C tender. The gradient post at the extreme left indicates why engines were needed front and rear of the train.

P J Robinson

dome. At slow speed it tended to stick. In mid-February 1954 a driver moving one of the newcomers around Ebbw Junction yard could not close his regulator and if the turntable had not luckily been set for his track would have dumped his 2–10–0 in the pit before he could manage to brake it. That flaw was corrected before the second batch of engines left Crewe.

The pinched design of the firebox to squeeze it above the rear driving wheels caused a problem or two, but ones that were soluble. Extra doors had to be cut into the ashpans of later engines to let disposal staff get at the ash and clinker which tended to build up in the flatter-than-normal slopes of the ashpan and threaten to jam and scar the rocking grate, and the exceptionally shallow main frames in this area needed strengthening.

The ten-coupled wheelbase, too, was troublesome for a while. To ease it round curves the BR designers had adopted Riddles' WD 2–10–0 scheme of flangeless centre drivers and thinner flanges than normal for the wheel on either side of it, which made the engine amenable to curves

53. One of the most celebrated of all class 9 2–10–0 stints – the Annesley–Woodford 'Windcutters' on the GC main line, a model of intensive steam locomotive utilisation: no. 92094, which appears to have had a severe water scaling problem, hurries coal south from Nottingham to Woodford near Ruschliffe Platform.

T G Hepburn/Rail Archive Stephenson

of even 100 yards' radius. At first, however, the flangeless wheel had an argument or two with high check rails. That was cured by a re-profiling of the tyres. After that the 2–10–0s were universally applauded as the sweetest-riding type in the whole standard range. 'Every 2–10–0 I have ridden,' wrote one LMR motive power man in 1960, 'has denied that there are any reciprocating masses at all, and there has been a complete absence of knock from axle-boxes or rods.'

It is not possible here to chronicle all the depots which operated 2–10–0s and the work to which they were put. The account has perforce to be limited to some of their outstanding

54. Titled train duty: class 9 2–10–0 no. 92069, with BR1F tender, wheels the up 'South Yorkshireman' past Kirkby South Junction, Notts., on 29 July 1958.

J Cupit

exploits and to the variations from standard design.

The first minor exception to normal 2–10–0 equipment was the 1955–6 fitting of ten engines, nos. 92060–6 and 92097–9, with a pair of air pumps, inserted at around the midpoint of the offside running plate, to activate the power operated doors of the special purpose hoppers on the North Eastern Region's Tyne Dock–Consett ore run. These were the halcyon years of the unfortunate Consett Iron Works. Following a considerable enlargement of the plant's capacity the Consett company of those days, the Tyne Improvement Commission and BR had collaborated to set up a forerunner of merry-go-round in November 1953.

New air-braked bogie hoppers, each 30 tons tare with a 56-ton payload capacity, and with power-operated discharge doors, were procured to maintain an intensive circuit working between overhead-loading bunkers at Tyne Dock and below-track discharge hoppers at Consett, so that the works could be fed with an average of 3,000 tons of ore daily. The 23 miles of railway included a 9-mile climb from Ouston to just beyond Annfield Plain, graded nearly the whole way at 1 in 35–65, so that this was one of the toughest – and the most spectacular – steam jobs in the NER. Before the 2–10–0s it was shared by specially pump-fitted ex-LNER class O1 2–8–0s and Q7 0–8–0s. One at the front and one banking at the rear, they were limited to eight hoppers and a brake, but with the 2–10–0s' advent loaded trains could be lengthened by a ninth hopper for a gross weight of just under 790 tons.

The most grotesque – and the one really ill-starred – 2–10–0 variant was the stud of ten fitted with Crosti boilers. In the immediate wake of the Second World War coal was a scarce and progressively more expensive fuel, so that a device claimed to have trimmed consumption by at least 20 per cent after application to numerous locomotives in its inventor's Italian homeland from 1940 onwards naturally intrigued the Railway Executive's team. The decision to give it a BR trial came late in the day, after the initial 2–10–0 production programme had been agreed. That accounts for the 1955 emergence of the Crosti-boilered 2–10–0s, nos. 92020–9, well past their slot in the Crewe numerical sequence.

Briefly summarised, the Crosti system sought extra work from the firebox gases. Instead of being ejected straight from the main boiler tubes to the atmosphere through a conventionally located chimney, they were curved back through a secondary drum or drums beneath the boiler so as to pre-heat the latter's feed water. From there they were directed to a final smokebox immediately ahead of the firebox, thence to be expelled through an ugly coal scuttle of a chimney extruding from the side of the boiler. The Italian and some of the DB engines in West Germany employing the system had two pre-heater drums, but the BR loading gauge dictated that the class 9 2–10–0s adopt the single-drum layout used on some Crosti-boiler-fitted class 50 2–10–0s of the DB. There was just room to squeeze the drum between boiler and driving axles because, with the Crosti system, it was claimed that a smaller main boiler would suffice to produce the same power output as that of the same locomotive type's conventionally boilered sisters. Italian Crosti engines had a naked smokebox top, but on the German and BR engines the ungainly look of the Crosti trappings was marginally alleviated by the concession of an orthodox chimney as help to draughting during lighting-up on shed.

The Italian concern which fathered the device seems to have had little doubt that BR's Crosti engines would delight their operators, since the deal with it provided for royalty payments scaled according to savings in coal consumption recorded when the variant had been submitted to a controlled test routine. The BR men must have been fairly euphoric too, as they were minded to try further Crosti boilers on some of the standard class 5 4–6–0s in the forward building programme. But that idea never left the pending file, though drawings survive to show what a top-heavy monstrosity it would have looked.

The Crostis were sent to work alongside a number of the first batch of orthodox class 9s that had been allocated to the Midland line's Wellingborough shed for the heavy freight hauls between Toton and Brent Sidings, London. Their reception was frosty from the start. Instant complaints that they were shy steamers by comparison with a standard class 9 were not

Cecil J Allen Collection

55. Crosti 2–10–0 under construction, showing how the pre-heater was squeezed beneath the boiler just above the driving axles.

stilled by an adjustment of blastpipe and chimney proportions that was certainly necessary, but that was the familiar enginemen's syndrome at work. The Midland men clearly could not get used to handling an engine that had some very novel characteristics. Obviously, a system that almost doubled the path of the firebox gases from grate to air reduced the power of exhaust draught and hence the brilliance of the fire. That seems to have misled many crews. Unconvinced that a Crosti was steaming properly they would pile on coal and give the engine the gun, with dire results because there would not be enough air in the firebox, the fire would choke and steam pressure slump.

On the German and Italian Crosti engines the final exhaust was carried like a grotesque organ pipe right up the boiler side to dome level. The cramping BR loading gauge, however, necessitated a much stumpier funnel on the class 9 2–10–0s; and that, coupled with the softer blast inherent in the arrangement, had the exhaust frequently swirling round the cab and as often as not being sucked into it, which made the Crosti 2–10–0s filthy engines to work. The fitting of

56. Crosti in full cry: no. 92025, blanketing its cab with exhaust, demonstrates why enginemen detested the Crosti-boilered engines as it heads southbound coal up the Midland main line past Trent.

T G Hepburn/Rail Archive Stephenson

deflectors to the side chimney did not eliminate the nuisance. Slimming of the blast nozzles was little more effective – and vitiated the whole purpose of the Crosti system by raising coal consumption.

To satisfy the terms of the contract with the Italians a Crosti and an orthodox 2–10–0 were squared up to each other with the formalities of a world title fight. The contest was over successive rounds on the Rugby Stationary Test Plant and on the road, the character of which had to be agreed in advance with an Italian State Railways traction engineer whom the Italian patentees had selected as their judge. Moreover, he had to be present throughout the trials and approve the verdicts of the ultimate report. Very much in evidence during the whole proceedings, too, was Dr Crosti himself. So far as the Italians were concerned, the purse was the full agreed rate of royalty if the Crosti contestant recorded a coal economy of 18 per cent or more over a standard 2–10–0 in predetermined conditions of working, with a rising scale of deductions as the advantage receded to 12 per cent, below which point the Italians were to forfeit their claim entirely.

Had the judges' decision been taken as final the Italians would have been left empty-handed. Within the agreed rules, no variation of working won the Crosti engine a better-than-8.4 per cent advantage over the standard 2–10–0. The crestfallen Italians naturally pressed for an exhaustive inquest and commissioned the great French designer André Chapelon, no less, to pick over every last detail of the test records.

At the end of the day the few certain reasons for the Italians' embarrassment started with the fact that BR – fortuitously, so it was said – had pitted a standard engine in sewing-machine order, no. 92050, against the Crosti no. 92023. Subsequent backroom comparisons of the latter's performance against the results obtained from no. 92013 in earlier routines at Rugby and over the Settle–Carlisle and ex-GSW main line in Scotland, yielded more points to the Crosti engine; in this paperwork confrontation, in fact, the Crosti did reach its 18 per cent savings target when it was being worked to the limit of a single fireman's capacity, since another conclusive deduction from the trials was that the Crosti system made its mark the harder the engines were driven. However, the Italians had agreed to wager on steaming and firing rates corresponding to the norm of BR's heavy freight operation. Suggestions that the Crosti process was not fully efficient in no. 92023 because of excessive scaling in its pre-heater drum were hard to credit, given that the engine had been dispatched almost straight from the Crewe assembly line to the Rugby Test Plant and had only 10,000 miles on the clock when the trials ended. Long after that correspondence was still flowing, until eventually the Italians agreed to accept a modest ex-gratia sum and regard the issue as closed but undecided.

What finally sealed the Crosti business on the BR side was a failing that also beset the German examples and aggravated their unpopularity there as well. In a conventional boiler the fire-tube gases were exhausted at a speed and temperature that kept the sulphur dioxide inevitably created in coal combustion from doing any damage on the way, even when an engine was on standby or being fired up. In the Crosti boilers of BR's 2–10–0s, however, the gases had frequently cooled to the point of reacting with the nitrous oxide products of combustion to condense as sulphuric acid by the time they reached the final exhaust chamber. This tendency was exacerbated by the high sulphur content of Belgian coal which the Midland sheds were using in the late 1950s as a result of long-term contracts concluded earlier in the decade during the national coal shortage (another outcome of which was that for some time the Toton–Brent coal traffic was two-way, Belgian imports northbound and East Midlands output southbound). The acid ate vicious holes in the smokebox and chimney, inflating maintenance and repair costs so intolerably that by the end of 1958 most of the Crosti 2–10–0s were side-tracked. Between 1959 and 1961 all ten were converted to a conventional layout by removal of the pre-heater drum and final exhaust apparatus, which left the small main boiler and diminutive smokebox-top chimney to do their normal job – though in this form they obviously had to be kept off duties that exacted a high boiler output. The rebuilds weighed 83.6 tons compared with the 86.7 ton norm of the class and 90.2 tons of a fully-rigged Crosti-boiler class 9F.

Just about the toughest freight assignments for any locomotive – or, for that matter, its crew

57. Crosti cleansed: rebuilt as an orthodox steam locomotive, no. 92024 heads oil tank empties past Leeds Holbeck in April 1967.

57 G W Morrison

– in the fading years of BR steam were the two daily merchandise trains operated over Ais Gill summit between the West Midlands and Carlisle, the 3.50 am and 4.45 pm from Water Orton yard and the 4.03 pm and 11.15 pm back from Carlisle. The distance was 226 miles and the end-to-end schedule five minutes short of seven hours. Each train was worked throughout by a Saltley engine, generally a Black Five 4–6–0 in the mid-1950s, which with a load up to its maximum of forty-three four-wheelers on a class D timing would eat its tender bare of coal if it had to battle with winter gales on the Pennine crossing.

By 1958 the 2–10–0s were already accepted as fast brake-fitted freight power. The ER's Great Northern operators, for instance, were using them interchangeably with class V2 2–6–2s on the already declining number of South Humberside fish trains; and in May that year one of the 2–10–0s had been allowed to romp down Stoke bank at almost 60 mph with 850 tons in tow in a loaded train test of the first 'Minfits', the vacuum-fitted vehicles that were intended to be BR's standard coal wagon, but had their career

58. Double-chimney class 9 2–10–0 no. 92223, with BR1G tender, heads southbound freight from its Carlisle base towards Leeds and is photographed between Skipton and Keighley in April 1967.

58 G W Morrison

terminated almost before it had begun by BR's withdrawal from wagonload coal traffic. A logical next step, therefore, was to see if the 2–10–0 could be made an even finer tool for this sort of work by fitting it with a mechanical stoker. So in mid-1958 nos. 92165–7 of Crewe's seventh lot were equipped with Berkley mechanical stokers (the specially-fitted tenders that went with them were classed BR1K) and allocated to Saltley depot for the Birmingham–Carlisle workings.

The objectives, through mechanically enabling the sustaining of a steaming rate in excess of one fireman's capacity over such a long run, was both to increase loads and tighten timings. With the advent of the stoker-fitted 2–10–0s the load limit was raised from 43 to 50 laden wagons on the class C fully brake-fitted workings and to 55 on the partially-fitted class D runs. But with BR's merchandise freight rapidly ebbing away these maxima were rarely attained in the dying years of steam traction, so that in practice the value of mechanical firing was seldom fully tested.

The other cardinal virtue of a mechanical stoker was its ability to feed a grate with inferior grades of coal dexterously enough for good combustion. But the mechanical stoker was a fussy eater. Its scroll feed could be choked by oversized lumps; and if the coal got too small and dusty the stoker's jets could easily dump it under the firebox arch, there to solidify unburnt, or propel it straight into the blast, to be sucked raw through the boiler tubes and sprayed over the trackside. Railways abroad with a substantial fleet of stoker-fired engines naturally laid on a supply of suitable fuel for them straight from the coalfields, but it took time for BR to organise a reserve of suitable coal for its three 2–10–0s at Saltley and Carlisle Canal sheds. For many months cleaners had to be mobilised at both depots to pick over the 2–10–0s' bunkers after they had been coaled and hack apart any lumps that looked oversized.

The Saltley enginemen obviously preferred the stoker-fitted 2–10–0s to the rest of the class 9s on their allocation, but controlled tests with one of the trio confirmed day-to-day evidence that British working conditions and locomotive size did not warrant mechanical firing. With good coal the stoker-fitted 2–10–0 could not surpass the steaming rate of a hand-fired 2–10–0, but consumed almost 25 per cent more fuel. With inferior coal the stoker certainly sustained a steaming rate beyond the reasonable limit of human firing, but again at a cost of 16 per cent greater fuel consumption. In neither case, however, did BR have duties consistently demanding continuous operation at such high rates of power output. With the arrival of class 45 diesels at Saltley late in 1961 the stoker-fitted 2–10–0s were laid aside. In the following year the stokers were dismantled, and as a hand-fired engine one of them, no. 92167, was the type's last survivor, scrapped in the summer of 1968.

The 1958 summer of the stoker-fitted 2–10–0s' debut was the first in which the class 9s raised eyebrows in passenger work. It started on the Great Central main line, where Annesley shed had been given a splendid stud of no fewer than forty-five 2–10–0s to extract last ounces of productivity from the celebrated Annesley–Woodford 'out-and-home' working. That sector of the GC route, just over 66 miles long, merged briefly two busy flows of cross-country freight, from the north-east to the south-west and from the East Midlands to South Wales. In 1947 the LNER had reorganised the daylong transfers of unfitted freight – about two dozen in each direction daily – between Annesley and Woodford yards into a strictly disciplined operation that guaranteed every locomotive and its crew would get in a return trip during one working shift. With the 2–10–0s – and the benefit of an admirably aligned route and a blind eye to the occasional 50 mph or even more despite the trains' innocence of continuous brakes – the working was intensified to secure quite a few double return trips totalling 266 miles per engine within 24 hours. In summer the Annesley–Woodford streams were swollen by extra passenger trains to and from the south and south-west coastal resorts, and the GC operators, usually reduced to purloining a 'foreign' V2 2–6–2 or B1 4–6–0 that happened to be on their premises to fulfil all their passenger commitments, realised in 1958 that the 2–10–0s were a feasible option.

The first 2–10–0 to hit memorable speed with a recorder on the train was no. 92164, in July 1958, when it was hitched on to the northbound 'Master Cutler' at Leicester. Urged up to 86 mph at the foot of the 1 in 176 descent to Ruddington, it put paid to the 23.4 miles from Leicester to Nottingham in just under even time start to stop.

That sparkling feat was eclipsed a month later on the East Coast main line. On Saturday 16 August King's Cross shed, drained of passenger power as it generally was around midday on a summer Saturday, turned out no. 92184 for the 1.45 pm King's Cross–Grantham semi-fast. The return leg of the diagram was the up 'Heart of Midlothian' and although Control besought Grantham shed to scour its yard for something more apt to complete the roster, as the ER General Manager was known to be aboard the express, Grantham could not oblige. No. 92184 it was that duly coupled up to the fourteen coaches and 485 tons gross of the 'HoM'.

Without a caning from signals at the approach to King's Cross they would have rolled in well ahead of time, for the 2–10–0 had incredibly passed Hatfield with over six minutes in hand, having touched 90 mph down Stoke bank, twice got pace as high as 78 mph on level track south of Peterborough, and accelerated to 76 mph on the slight slope beyond Welwyn. And that without a scent of overheating, despite driving wheels of only 5 ft diameter – which, incidentally, cast more doubt on the need of roller-bearing main axles; the 2–10–0s' roller bearings were confined to their tenders. Some experts contended that the 2–10–0s rode so superbly drivers had no inkling of the speeds they were attaining.

The frowns railway periodical publicity for this exploit elicited in high places restrained 2–10–0 drivers for a while, though throughout the 1959 summer the WR added its 2–10–0s to the list of suitable power for calculated rostering to summer Saturday passenger extras on both Plymouth–Penzance and South Wales main lines from Paddington. And when the last of the line, no. 92220, 'Evening Star', was delivered to Cardiff Canton, its GW-like livery, with the crowning glory of a copper-capped chimney, could hardly be insulted by the engine's confinement to freight duty. In fact, it was quite regularly deputed to secondary passenger work. And it was from a Cardiff–Salisbury passenger stint that it was appropriated on 27 June 1960 as a last-minute replacement for a defective Britannia on the up 'Red Dragon'.

The Cardiff Canton driver quickly took to his stop-gap, so much so that on the return leg of the diagram with the westbound 'Capitals United Express' from Paddington he guessed that he had spurred 'Evening Star' up to 80 mph, and probably more, on the falling grades to the Severn Tunnel. That prompted the deliberate rostering of the 2–10–0 to the same turn on a number of days in the ensuing three weeks. Sadly, news of the 2–10–0's elevation to the purple penetrated BR headquarters, whereupon blistering reproofs descended on the Canton offices and 'Evening Star's' top link forays were at an end.

That same year some 2–10–0s were officially assigned to one sphere of passenger work that made the most of their characteristics and capability. The ferociously graded Somerset & Dorset line over the Mendips, slumping deeper into operating deficit by the year, desperately needed a modern all-purpose type with sufficient brake power for the line's freight (a criterion neither the BR standard class 5 4–6–0 nor the WD 2–8–0 had met) and the virility to reduce, if not eliminate, the double-heading of summer passenger trains. SR misgivings at the effect of 2–10–0s on track at their end of S&D line were overcome, and at the end of March 1960 no. 92204, one of the Bristol St Philips Marsh allocation, was tested between Bath and Bournemouth West with an eleven-coach train of 350 tons. Its unassisted performance in filthy conditions, with driving rain degenerating to snow in the Mendips, was a triumph, and in the following June four 2–10–0s were added to the Bath Green Park shed allocation for regular work on this cross-country route.

The class 9s were fully extended over the S&D line for only three summers, since at the conclusion of the 1962 high season the first

J M Jarvis/Colourviews Ltd

59. The sole Giesl-ejector-fitted 2–10–0, no. 92250.

move towards closure of the Mendips railway was taken with the diversion to other routes of all its long-haul trains. That summer 'Evening Star' was specially drafted to Bath so that it could dignify the last 'Pines Express' to take the S&D route in August (though it returned to take a hand in the residual Bath–Bournemouth stopping service the following summer). But the 2–10–0s had enough time in the Mendips to record there some of the outstanding performances in their generally impressive career.

One of the finest to see print was put up by double-chimney no. 92000 in July 1961 with a twelve-coach southbound 'Pines Express' taring 416 tons, slightly exceeding the official class 9 unassisted limit of 410 tons over the route, and grossing about 450 tons. Slowed to 50 mph for the single-line tablet exchange at Corfe Mullen Junction, the 2–10–0, thundering defiance on full regular and 45 per cent cut-off, dropped only 7 mph on the ensuing two miles of 1 in 80 up, its cylinders and steam passages freely processing steam at a rate well above the boiler's ability to produce it for any lengthy period

60. Last of the line: class 9 2–10–0 no. 92220, the green-liveried 'Evening Star', takes an outing from the National Railway Museum at York to Scarborough on 4 July 1976 and is photographed on the return at Castle Howard.

P J Robinson

of time. Further south, on the 1½ miles of Parkstone bank's 1 in 60, speed dropped from an initial 47 mph only to 41 mph as the driver gave the 2–10–0 52 per cent cut-off.

The start of 1961 saw 2–10–0s allocated to an SR shed for the first time. To cope with the fast-developing oil traffic from the Fawley refinery to the West Midlands distribution railhead at Bromford Bridge via Salisbury, Westbury and Bristol nos. 92204–6/31/7 were delivered to Eastleigh depot.

One last 2–10–0 experiment was the 1959 fitting of no. 92250 with a Giesl oblong ejector in place of its double blastpipe and chimney. Another device calculated to reduce coal consumption, but in this case also to extend a locomotive's capability beyond its known steaming limits with an orthodox exhaust, Dr Giesl-Gieslingen's invention had been remarkably successful in numerous applications to engines of his national railway system, the Austrian Federal. In brief, it associated a tier of blast nozzles with a single, oblong, tapering chimney as a means to accelerate the gases from the fire-tubes, and narrow the speed gap between them and the exhaust steam from the cylinders, with the object of reducing back pressure and improving draught. The National Coal Board had a keen interest in BR's attitude to the Giesl ejector, for the latter was said to make possible the efficient use of coal grades previously inconceivable as steam locomotive fuel and the NCB had plenty of them looking for a buyer.

The controlled tests of no. 92250 were schemed, agreed and conducted with the same punctilio as those of the Crosti boiler, and with similar provision for royalty payments. But though the efficacy of the Giesl ejector in ideal working conditions was fully proved, the trials with inferior coal were chequered, and the savings in consumption insufficient to offset the difficulties encountered in firing with the poorer grades. Moreover, the NCB could not offer the latter at as low a price as some had expected. Consequently no. 92250 remained the solitary Giesl-ejector engine of the class.

Perhaps the greatest tragedy of all wrought by BR's pell-mell dieselisation was the incredibly early slaughter of the superbly efficient 2–10–0s. The first withdrawals in 1964 included six engines that had been rolled out of Crewe only six years earlier. But happily private enterprise has seen to it that the 2–10–0s were not obliterated by the final withdrawals of 1968.

Examples preserved:

Class 9 2–10–0 nos.

92203	East Somerset Railway
92212	Great Central Main Line Trust
92214	Peak Railway Society
92220	National Railway Museum
92240	Bluebell Railway

Appendix 1

BR Standard Steam Locomotives: Leading Particulars

Type	*Number Series*	*Boiler Type*	*Driving Wheel Diameter*	*Boiler Barrel Outside Diameter*	*Firebox Outside*	*Heating Surfaces*			*Length between Tubeplates*	*Grate Area*	*Cylinders*	*Tractive Effort*	*Weight in Working Order*
						Tubes	*Firebox*	*Super-heater*					
Class 8 4–6–2	71000	BR13	6′ 2″	5′ 9″ to 6′ 5 1/2″	8′ 0 1/8″ long 7′ 9″ to 7′ 4″ wide	2264 sq.′	226 sq.′	691 sq.′	17′	48.6 sq.′	18″×28″ (3)	39,080 lb	101 tons 5 cwt
Class 7 4–6–2	70000	BR1	6′ 2″	5′ 9″ to 6′ 5 1/2″	7′ long 7′ 9″ to 7′ 4″ wide	2264 sq.′	210 sq.′	677 sq.′	17′	42 sq.′	20″×28″	32,150 lb	94 tons
Class 6 4–6–2	72000	BR2	6′ 2″	5′ 4″ to 6′ 1″	6′ 9″ long 7′ to 6′ 8″ wide	1878 sq.′	195 sq′	592 sq.′	17′	36 sq.′	19 1/2″×28″	27,520 lb	88 tons 10 cwt
Class 5 4–6–0	73000	BR3	6′ 2″	4′ 11 11/16″ to 5′ 8 1/2″	9′ 2 13/16″ long 3′ 11 7/8″ wide	1479 sq.′	171 sq.′	358 sq.′	13′ 2 7/8″	28.7 sq.′	19″×28″	26,120 lb	76 tons
Class 4 4–6–0	75000	BR4	5′ 8″	4′ 9″ to 5′ 3″	8′ 6″ long 4′ 0 1/2″ wide	1301 sq.′	143 sq.′	258 sq.′	13′	26.7 sq.′	18″×28″	25,515 lb	67 tons 18 cwt
Class 4 2–6–0	76000	BR7	5′ 3″	4′ 9″ to 5′ 3″	7′ 6″ long 4′ 0 1/2″ wide	1075 sq.′	131 sq.′	247 sq.′	10′ 10 1/2″	23 sq.′	17 1/2″×26″	24,170 lb	59 tons 15 cwt
Class 4 2–6–4T	80000	BR5	5′ 8″	4′ 9″ to 5′ 3″	8′ 6″ long 4′ 0 1/2″ wide	1223 sq.′	143 sq.′	240 sq.′	12′ 3″	26.7 sq.′	18″×28″	25,515 lb	86 tons 13 cwt
Class 3 2–6–0	77000	BR6	5′ 3″	4′ 5″ to 5′ 0 1/2″	7′ long 4′ wide	923.5 sq.′	118.4 sq.′	184.5 sq.′	10′ 10 1/2″	20.4 sq.′	17 1/2″×26″	21,490 lb	57 tons 10 cwt
Class 3 2–6–2T	82000	BR6	5′ 3″	4′ 5″ to 5′ 0 1/2″	7′ long 4′ wide	923.5 sq.′	118.4 sq.′	184.5 sq.′	10′ 10 1/2″	20.4 sq.′	17 1/2″×26″	21,490 lb	74 tons 1 cwt
Class 2 2–6–0	78000	BR8	5′	4′ 3″ to 4′ 8″	5′ 11″ long 4′ 0 7/16″ wide	924 sq.′	101 sq.′	124 sq.′	10′ 10 1/2″	17.5 sq.′	16 1/2″×24″	18,513 lb	49 tons 5 cwt
Class 2 2–6–2T	84000	BR8	5′	4′ 3″ to 4′ 8″	5′ 11″ long 4′ 0 7/16″ wide	924 sq.′	101 sq.′	124 sq.′	10′ 10 1/2″	17.5 sq.′	16 1/2″×24″	18,513 lb	66 tons 5 cwt
Class 9 2–10–0	92000	BR9	5′	5′ 9″ to 6′ 1″	7′ 5 1/4″ long 7′ 0 1/8″ to 6′ 6 7/16″ wide	1836 sq.′	179 sq.′	535 sq.′	15′ 3″	40.2 sq.′	20″×28″	39,667 lb	86 tons 14 cwt

Appendix 2

BR Standard Steam Locomotive Tender Types

	Capacity		*Weight in full WO*	
Type	*Water galls*	*Coal tons*	*tons*	*cwt*
BR1	4,250	7	49	3
BR1A	5,000	7	52	10
BR1B	4,725	7	50	5
BR1C	4,725	9	53	5
BR1D	4,725	9	54	10
BR1E	4,725	10	55	10
BR1F	5,625	7	55	5
BR1G	5,000	7	52	10
BR1H	4,250	7	49	3
BR1J	4,325	10	53	14
BR1K	4,325	9	52	7
BR2	3,500	6	42	3
BR2A	3,500	6	42	3
BR3	3,000	4	36	17

Appendix 3

Construction Dates and Locomotive Works Responsible

Class	*Batch*	*Building Works*	*Year*	*Class*	*Batch*	*Building Works*	*Year*
7 4–6–2	70000–24	Crewe	1951		76100–14	Doncaster	1957
	70025–44	Crewe	1952–3	3 2–6–0	77000–19	Swindon	1954
	70045–54	Crewe	1954	2 2–6–0	78000–9	Darlington	1952–3
6 4–6–2	72000–9	Crewe	1951–2		78010–9	Darlington	1953–4
8 4–6–2	71000	Crewe	1954		78020–54	Darlington	1954
5 4–6–0	73000–9	Derby	1951		78055–64	Darlington	1956
	73010–29	Derby	1951–2	4 2–6–4T	80000–9	Derby	1951
	73030–9	Derby	1952–3		80010–30	Brighton	1951–2
	73040–9	Derby	1953		80031–53	Brighton	1952
	73050–74	Derby	1954		80054–8	Derby	1954–5
	73075–99	Derby	1955		80059–80	Brighton	1953–4
	73100–24	Doncaster	1955–6		80081–105	Brighton	1954–5
	73125–44	Derby	1956		80106–15	Doncaster	1954
	73145–54	Derby	1957		80116–30	Brighton	1955
	73155–71	Doncaster	1956–7		80131–44	Brighton	1956
4 4–6–0	75000–9	Swindon	1951		80145–54	Brighton	1954/6
	75010–9	Swindon	1951–2	3 2–6–2T	82000–19	Swindon	1952
	75020–9	Swindon	1952–3		82020–44	Swindon	1954–5
	75030–49	Swindon	1953–4	2 2–6–2T	84000–19	Crewe	1953
	75050–64	Swindon	1955–6		84020–9	Darlington	1957
	75065–79	Swindon	1956–7	9 2–10–0	92000–19	Crewe	1954
4 2–6–0	76000–4	Horwich	1952		92020–9	Crewe	1955
	76005–19	Horwich	1952–3		92030–49	Crewe	1954–5
	76020–4	Doncaster	1952–3		92050–86	Crewe	1955–6
	76025–9	Doncaster	1953		92087–96	Swindon	1956–7
	76030–44	Doncaster	1953–4		92097–134	Crewe	1956–7
	76045–69	Doncaster	1955–6		92135–77	Crewe	1957–8
	76070–4	Doncaster	1956		92178–202	Swindon	1957–8
	76075–89	Horwich	1956–7		92203–20	Swindon	1959–60
	76090–9	Horwich	1957		92221–50	Crewe	1958

Index

Air-braked wagon trials, Toton–Brent 31, 59
Allen, Cecil J. 26
Automatic Warning System 29, 83

Barnes, Alfred Rt Hon 20
Bluebell Railway 68, 88, 105
Bressingham Museum 37
Brighton works 19, 76
'Broadsman', The 27

Cab design, Driving 21
Cameron of Lochiel 40
'Capitals United Express', The 102
Caprotti poppet valve gear 45, 55, 59
Chappel Steam Centre 88
Churchill, Winston 29
Cock, C. F. 44
Consett Iron Works 94
'Coronation Scot', The 25
Cox, E. S. 16, 44
Crewe Works 24, 36, 46, 88, 91
Cripps, Sir Stafford 15
Crosti boiler 95 *et seq*

Darlington works 74
Dart Valley Railway 88
'Deltic' diesel locomotive 48
Derby works 19, 44, 51, 76
Diesel schemes, LMS and LNER 16
Doncaster works 19, 51, 69, 76
Double blastpipe and chimney 20, 45, 65, 89
Dymond, A. W. J. 17

East Somerset Railway 68, 105

Ell, S. O. 65
Exchanges, Locomotive, 1948 16, 17, 38, 49

Festival of Britain, 1951 27

General Election, 1951 29
Giesl Oblong Ejector 105
Gingell, Driver Sam 57
'Golden Arrow', The 27
Great Central Main Line Trust, The 105
Great Western Railway locomotives:
'Castle' 4–6–0 29
'County' 4–6–0 38
'Hall' 4–6–0 38
'Manor' 4–6–0 57
51XX, 81XX 2–6–2T 62
56XX 0–6–2T 62

Hardy, R. H. N. 27
Harrison, J. F. 44
Harrow & Wealdstone collision 44
Horwich works 69
Hurcomb, Lord 15

Isle of Wight Railways 88
Ivatt, H. G. 51, 69

Keighley & Worth Valley Railway 68, 75, 88

Last Steam Special, BR 37
Liveries, locomotive 19, 55, 91
LMS locomotive classes:
'Duchess' 4–6–2 21, 43, 44
'Princess Royal' 4–6–2 44, 48

'Royal Scot' 4–6–0 18, 20, 33, 35, 43
'Jubilee' 4–6–0 35, 38, 41, 43
Class 5 4–6–0 38, 41, 51, 55, 62, 76
8F 2–8–0 89
4 2–6–4T 63, 76
3 2–6–2T 85
LNER locomotive classes:
A1 4–6–2 32, 89
A2 4–6–2 33, 44, 89
A3 4–6–2 50
A4 4–6–2 50, 69
B1 4–6–0 38, 58, 59
B17 4–6–0 53
K1 2–6–0 59
L1 2–6–4T 59
O1 2–8–0 95
P2 2–8–2 48
Q7 0–8–0 95
V2 2–6–2 20, 33, 43, 54, 58, 59, 99
Locomotive Standards Committee 17

Main Line Steam Trust 48
Market Bosworth Light Railway 75
'Master Cutler', The 101
Mechanical stoker, Berkley 100
'Mid-day Scot', The 46
Mid-Hants Railway 75
Midland Railway Trust, Butterley 68
Milton accident 29
Minfit wagons 99
Missenden, Sir Eustace 15, 20
Mobile test units 55
Modernisation Plan, BR 1955 41
Morrison, Herbert 15
Motive Power Depots, BR:
Accrington 64
Annesley 101
Ashford 84, 88
Aston 35, 43
Barry 86
Basingstoke 68
Bath 84, 102
Bedford 64
Blackpool 52
Blaydon 59
Bletchley 64, 81, 88
Bolton 88
Brighton 68
Bristol St Philips Marsh 54, 102
Bury 81
Camden 28
Cardiff Canton 29, 64, 102
Carlisle Canal 101
Carlisle Kingmoor 39
Chester 52, 54, 64, 86
Corkerhill 81
Crewe North 46
Cricklewood 71
Darlington 69, 73
Derby 59
Doncaster 75
Dover 68, 84
Eastfield 58
Eastleigh 69, 87, 104
Ebbw Junction 91
Exmouth Junction 68, 84, 87
Feltham 87
Fleetwood 88
Gateshead 69
Glasgow Polmadie 31, 39, 81, 84
Glasgow St Rollox 62
Grantham 102
Hamilton 74
Hawick 75
Haymarket 42
Holbeck 28, 33, 59
Holyhead 30, 35
Hull Dairycoates 73, 88
Hurlford 74
Kentish Town 81, 88
King's Cross 58
Kittybrewster 71, 81
Laira 28
Llandudno Junction 35
Longsight 37
Malton 88
March 35, 71, 74, 87
Motherwell 67, 75
Neasden 35, 55, 71, 83
Neville Hill 83
Newton Abbot 86
Newton Heath 35, 43, 81
Nine Elms 54, 87
Norwich 25, 30, 35
Old Oak Common 28
Oswestry 64, 74
Oxford 64
Oxley 36
Patricroft 52, 59
Perth South 52
Ramsgate 88
Redhill 69
Salisbury 69
Saltley 100
Scarborough 73
Sheffield Darnall 58
Shrewsbury 54, 55, 59
Southport 68
St Margarets 84
Stewarts Lane 33, 56, 84
Stoke 71
Stratford 20, 30, 35, 42

Stranraer 71
Swansea East Dock 83
Swansea Landore 55
Three Bridges 68
Trafford Park 33
Treherbert 86
Tunbridge Wells West 80
Tyseley 86
Watford 81
Wellingborough 95
Wellington 86
West Auckland 74
Weymouth 84
Whitby 83
Wrexham 86
York 58, 59, 73

National Railway Museum 105
Nene Valley Railway 37, 68
'Night Scotsman', The 42
North Staffordshire Railway Society 88
North Yorkshire Moors Railway 88

'Palatine', The 33
Parker, L. P. 27
Peak Railway Society 88, 105

'Pines Express', The 103
'Queen of Scots', The 42

Railway Executive 23, 27, 52, 78
'Red Dragon', The 102
Riddles, R. A. 15, 32, 37, 44, 89
Roller bearings 32
Rugby Test Plant 24, 55, 97

Scottish Railway Preservation Society 88
Severn Valley Railway 37, 53, 68, 75, 88
Southern Railway locomotive classes:
Bulleid 4–6–2 20, 23, 27, 32, 41, 46
N15 4–6–0 56
W 2–6–4T 79
Steamport, Southport 75
Swindon works 19, 47, 63, 65, 85, 90

'Thames–Clyde Express', The 28

WD 2–8–0 class 89
WD 2–10–0 class 92
Weir electrification report 15
'West Coast Postal', The 46
Woodhams, Barry 48